CONDUCTING STAFF APPRAISALS

If you want to know how . . .

Writing a CV that works
How to develop and use your key marketing tool

Planning a Career Change
Rethink your way to a better working life

Passing that Interview
Your step-by-step guide to coming out on top

Succeeding at Interviews
How to give great answers and ask the right questions

howtobooks

For full details, please send for a free copy of the
latest catalogue:

How To Books
Spring Hill House, Spring Hill Road, Begbroke
Oxford OX5 1RX, United Kingdom
info@howtobooks.co.uk
www.howtobooks.co.uk

REVISED AND UPDATED · SIXTH EDITION · 6

CONDUCTING
STAFF
APPRAISALS

How to set up a
review system that
really will improve
individual
performance and
organisational
results

Dr NIGEL HUNT

howtobooks

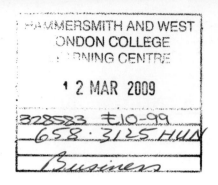
Published by How To Books Ltd,
Spring Hill House, Spring Hill Road, Begbroke
Oxford OX5 1RX, United Kingdom.
Tel: (01865) 375794. Fax: (01865) 379162.
info@howtobooks.co.uk
www.howtobooks.co.uk

Sixth edition 2007

British Library Cataloguing in Publication Data
A catalogue record for this book is available from the British
Library

ISBN: 978 1 84528 213 4

Cover design by Baseline Arts Ltd, Oxford
Produced for How To Books by Deer Park Productions,
Tavistock
Typeset by TW Typesetting, Plymouth, Devon
Printed and bound by Cromwell Press, Trowbridge, Wiltshire

NOTE: The material contained in this book is set out in good
faith for general guidance and no liability can be accepted for
loss or expense incurred as a result of relying in particular
circumstances on statements made in the book. The laws and
regulations are complex and liable to change, and readers
should check the current position with the relevant
authorities before making personal arrangements.

Contents

Preface   ix

1 **Integrated staff appraisals**   **1**
   What is the purpose of staff appraisal?   3
   Why bother with appraisal?   6
   Training the appraiser, training the appraisee   8
   Size of organisation   8
   The open organisation   9
   The 360 degree appraisal   11
   Ethical issues   11
   Straightforward design   12
   What can go wrong with appraisal?   13
   The structure of the book   17

2 **The open organisation and appraisal**   **20**
   The open organisation   20
   What is openness?   23
   Information that should be available   25
   Transparency and openness   27
   Good reasons for secrecy   28
   Anxieties and issues about appraisal and the open
     organisation   29
   Commitment   37
   So why do appraisals fail?   38
   Concluding comments   40

3 **The purposes of appraisal**   **41**
   The various purposes   41
   Timing   43
   Motivation   43

Appraisal is for the employer as well as the
   employee   45
Performance review   45
Training and development   50
Promotion and transfer   52
Assessing potential   53
Vocational guidance   55
Personal health   56
Team development   58
Job redesign   59
Integrating objectives   61
Addressing problem areas   61
Case study   63

4   People and appraisal skills   66
Who should conduct staff appraisals?   67
Appraisal skills   71
Interviewing skills   73
Listening skills   74
The purposes of the interview   76
Finding background information   77
Preparing for the interview   78
Basic counselling skills   80
Negotiating skills   81
Job analysis   88
Other important skills   90
Case study   93

5   Describing the job, describing the person   96
Introduction to job descriptions   97
Job analysis   99
Job description   105
The person specification   108
Appraisal, job description and person
   specification   114
Case study   116

6 Alternative appraisals   **118**
Types of appraisal   118
Pay-related appraisal   118
Self-appraisal   122
Peer appraisal   124
Upward appraisals   128
Timing appraisals: regular vs continuous   131
Concluding comments   132

7 The 360 degree appraisal   **133**
What is a 360 degree appraisal?   133
When should organisations use 360 degree
  appraisals?   137
Benefits of the 360 degree appraisal   140
When should you not use 360 degree appraisal?   141
The practicalities of the 360 degree appraisal   143
Problems and solutions   147
Job description/person specification   151
Concluding comments   152

8 Preparation   **153**
Using performance criteria   154
Supervisor, peer and upward ratings   158
Performance against previous objectives   165
Psychometric measures   167
Choosing which data to collect   173
The pre-appraisal report   174
Understanding your opposite number   178
Preparing for the interview   179

9 Conducting the interview   **182**
Preparing for the interview   182
Interview scheduling   183
Choosing the place for the interview   186
Conducting the interview   187

Appraising under-performers and staff with
   problems   192
After the interview   193
Case study   197

10 Evaluation   **200**
Following up   202
Validating the appraisal system   205
How appraisal can be unfair   212
Identifying sources of conflict   216
Case study   217

11 Present thoughts and future directions   **220**
What is the state of appraisal?   221
Work-home balance   224
Legal and ethical issues   225
Appraising professional and scientific staff   225
The problem with staff appraisal   229
Conclusions   230

Glossary   **232**

Useful addresses   **240**

Index   **243**

Preface

This is the sixth edition of a book first published in 1992. This edition has been updated to take into account continuing changes in appraisal and performance review practice. The philosophy behind the book is that the open organisation is crucial to a successful appraisal system. For an open organisation, appraisal is generally a two way process, with both parties genuinely interested in an effective organisation and a satisfied employee.

The book continues to provide practical help with designing appraisal systems, including understanding the purposes of the appraisal, deciding who should be the appraiser, acquiring appropriate skills, devising job descriptions and person specifications, conducting the interview, and follow up and validation. The book uses illustrations, bullet points, case studies and discussion points to highlight the main issues.

It is a practical guide to appraisal.

$$1$$

Integrated staff appraisals

In this chapter:

◆ **What is the purpose of staff appraisal?**

◆ **The open organisation**

◆ **Ethical issues**

◆ **What can go wrong?**

◆ **Structure of the book**

In a recent survey, 50 per cent of employers said they carried out appraisal annually, with 41 per cent holding appraisal meetings more frequently: 14 per cent saying they had quarterly appraisals.

This book is written for people who are involved in staff appraisal now, and those who are intending to become so in the future. This includes the employer in the small to medium size company who wishes to implement or improve an appraisal system, the human resource manager in the larger company who wonders why their expensive staff appraisal system does not appear to be working, anyone who carries out appraisals, management students, and not least people who are being appraised. The book provides practical advice on the general conditions in which an appraisal should take place, appropriate training for the appraiser and appraisee, and the means by which to design and implement the appraisal.

Some organisations and employees continue to view appraisal negatively; it takes up (or wastes) time, resources and energy. The purpose of an organisation – they claim – is not to do appraisals; an organisation exists to make money or, in the case of public organisations such as schools, universities, the social services and the health service, provide a good service. Good employees will usually give full priority to production, whatever the nature of the product or service. Appraisal is not seen as having a direct connection to production. This is a fallacious argument. Appraisal, well managed, enables the organisation to be aware of what the individual is doing, and the individual to be aware that their contribution is valued and, importantly, that they will receive some reward.

WHAT IS THE PURPOSE OF STAFF APPRAISAL?

The purposes of staff appraisal are manifold, but the main thing is that both the employer and the employee should be satisfied; the employer should be satisfied that the employee is functioning well in terms of the needs of the organisation; the employee should be satisfied that the employer and the organisation are looking after their needs.

But what do we mean by need? Need is a difficult and ambiguous term which means very different things to people – especially when those people are employers and employees, who have traditionally sat on opposite sides of the fence, but who should be working in a cooperative venture.

The employer needs the employee to:

◆ turn up on time and do a full day's work;

◆ work effectively and efficiently;

◆ generate profit.

The employee needs the employer to provide:

◆ a safe and pleasant working environment;

- appropriate opportunities for training and development;

- other suitable motivators, eg money, annual leave, flexibility.

They both need a little give and take; the employee might book a holiday using the company's internet, but they take work home at night and use their own printing facilities.

Staff appraisal is one means by which both the employer and the employee try to ensure that their respective needs are satisfied. Unfortunately, in many organisations the staff appraisal system leaves a lot to be desired. It is neither efficient nor does it satisfy needs; and no one really takes much notice of it. This is true in organisations which take a perfunctory view of appraisal, either not bothering at all or just having the odd informal interview – perhaps in a corridor; 'How are you getting on Phil?' kind of discussion. It is also true in organisations that attempt to implement detailed and effective appraisal systems where the appraisal is fully prepared for, carried out in detail, and does not consist just of one interview in a year. The problem with the former is plain to see, so what is the problem with the latter?

Problems of effective staff appraisal

The problem with many organisations, and this is particularly true of large organisations, is that even when they have detailed appraisal policies, the follow up is not effective. Many employees do not take appraisal seriously because they know that, for instance, if a training need has been identified, the organisation will often ignore the recommendation and will not implement what has been agreed. Alternatively, the appraiser may not have the authority to make promises regarding training needs and has to refer it to a higher authority. Through bureaucratisation the appraisal system fails. The end result is that the individual appraisee feels that the organisation is just paying lip service to the appraisal system – and the truth is, it is. The organisation has the appraisal system because it feels it should do, rather than because there are good reasons for implementing such a system.

How many organisations that you have worked in are like this? Appraisal is simply not taken seriously. Years of research shows appraisal can improve the productivity of the organisation and the satisfaction of the individual employee when carried out effectively, yet organisations still do not take it seriously.

There are a number of reasons why this may be so. We are all a little averse to bureaucracy – form filling – we just can't be bothered. There are some organisations which genuinely do not care about their employees. There are employees who do not care about – or trust – their organisation. The way round this is the *open organisation*; working in an organisation which involves the individual employee at all levels, which consults over major decisions, recognises the home-work relationship, and ultimately respects the needs of the individual. This is discussed in detail in the next chapter. For now it is enough to point out that appraisal will not be truly effective except in the open organisation.

WHY BOTHER WITH APPRAISAL?

Appraisal can help the organisation be more efficient (and hence profitable), and also help the individual employee gain more job satisfaction. A satisfied employee is going to work better; a more profitable company means a happier boss. Easy!

Appraisals are carried out for a range of reasons. These can include:

◆ performance review;

◆ assessing training needs;

◆ determining job change (promotion or role change);

thing whereby the employer or the employee have needs relating to each other.

The performance review is important in a staff appraisal; because the employer wants to ensure that the employee is working effectively, and has carried out their tasks at an appropriate level of performance. Performance review generally works against a set of objectives that will have been agreed at a previous staff appraisal. In an ideal world the employee will have attained – or preferably exceeded – these targets. This is fine for the employer, but the needs of the employee may be different. The employee may be more concerned about training and development needs, or needs relating to family and leisure. They may wish to take on different tasks in their job for which they need training. They may wish to alter their working hours to take into account changes in their family circumstances (life is not just a rat race). Perhaps they would like promotion, or to move to another role. It is important that the employee has the opportunity to explore these issues in the appraisal.

Longer term career goals and expectations may need to be explored. Where does the employee want to be in five or ten years? How do they hope to get there? These are not trivial questions – neither is the reply 'In your shoes' to the boss a trivial reply though it is rather

clichéd and best not used for that reason! The appraisal should also be used for counselling the employee
regarding performance issues, training and development issues, and longer term career goal issues.

TRAINING THE APPRAISER, TRAINING THE APPRAISEE

In many organisations it is thought that appraisal is a
straightforward task that can be carried out by anyone,
such as a junior member of the human resources team
or a recently appointed supervisor. It is not; it requires
a range of skills and attributes. The appraiser must
have negotiating skills, counselling skills, bargaining
skills. They may need to be aware of company law, of
what they can offer by way of training, etc. The
appraisee should also have some of these skills. They
too need to know how to negotiate and bargain, in
order to get the best individual deal. These issues will
be explored in a later chapter.

SIZE OF ORGANISATION

Some people think that it is only larger organisations
that can and should have an appraisal system. While it
is the case that larger organisations are in a better
position to afford a sophisticated and efficient system,
organisations of all sizes, down to the smaller company
with just a few employees, should have some sort of
system. It is important for employers to be in touch

with the needs and feelings of their employees. Discontent breeds resentment, which leads to the loss of good staff. For the employee, it is important that they feel needed by the organisation, that the organisation respects them.

THE OPEN ORGANISATION

Feeling needed is a particular difficulty in larger organisations that, because of their size, are often impersonal. It may be difficult or impossible for more junior staff to have much or any contact with senior management. It may be rare for senior managers to interact with junior staff. While this is bound to happen it does not benefit either side. This is why an appraisal system is most effective when it is linked, particularly in a larger organisation, with an open management system.

'Open' means a number of things, including openness of information. We in the UK now – supposedly – have what is called open government. While in many ways this is a misnomer, it is true that we have more access to more information about a wider range of topics than ever before. We have the right to know what ministers have written in their memos to civil servants, the right to know what is being discussed in cabinet, the right to know what information government organisations hold on us. While there are many exceptions to this openness – for example where state security is concerned – people feel better for knowing that they can find out what our government is up to. The same applies to large companies. The more junior members of staff are aware of what is happening in the organisation the more satisfied they will generally feel.

In the end employees will feel more part of the organisation if they are kept informed of what is happening. That is why it is important to recognise that a good staff appraisal system can only occur in an open organisation. Turning the argument back on its head, it is clear that many sophisticated staff appraisals do not work, not because they are poor appraisal systems in themselves, but because they are not integrated into the open organisation.

The problem with employers and the open organisation

Too many employers believe that an open organisation will cause problems. There are a number of reasons why this might be. For instance psychologists have explored reasons why individuals and groups (including organisations) may feel insecure. The release of knowledge or information can make people feel vulnerable. Employers who release information to their employees may feel insecure and threatened; they may feel their own position is at risk if they disclose information to employees. Secrecy is power.

THE 360 DEGREE APPRAISAL

This brings us to a relatively new concept, that of the 360 degree appraisal. This entails obtaining ratings from a range of people who have contact with the appraisee, including line managers and supervisors, colleagues doing the same job, subordinates, and possibly customers or others outside the organisation. The 360 degree appraisal enables a broader assessment of the appraisee and their relationships with others. There are a number of problems with the 360 degree appraisal, which are examined in Chapter 7. For such a system to work effectively, it is important for the organisation to be open. The 360 degree appraisal is not appropriate for all organisations, but it should be considered as a possibility.

ETHICAL ISSUES

All appraisal systems should be ethical, they should be fair to all parties involved in the appraisal system. The organisation should not open itself to charges of unfair treatment, whether to do with legal issues such as sex, age, or race discrimination, or general matters of fairness across staff, such as access to training and development and promotion. The system should not just be concerned with legal issues, but with moral and ethical ones too.

The appraisal *system* should also be fair to everyone involved in the system. That is not to say that all employees should receive the same kind of appraisal; that may not be appropriate, but that within the system all are treated equally. The same procedures and guidelines should be used for everyone, and the same means of evaluating the system. If the system is well designed, then this will not present a problem.

Ethics is also about openness. We will consider the open organisation in detail in the next chapter, but openness also concerns the ways people treat each other. The appraiser should be open with the appraisee. For instance, do not promise training if you know it will not be available, do not make any promises you cannot keep.

STRAIGHTFORWARD DESIGN

An appraisal system should be as simple as possible. It should not be over-bureaucratic. Employees will not take kindly to complex forms containing many management-speak questions. Also, the bureaucracy of the system should be minimised. It is not necessary to produce forms in triplicate to be sent to various departments who will file them away and never look at them. Unless there is good reason, the only people to see the appraisal forms will be – and should be – the appraiser and the appraisee. This becomes a little more complicated when there are multiple quantitative forms, and this is dealt with in a later chapter.

WHAT CAN GO WRONG WITH APPRAISAL?

It is useful from the outset to think about the reasons why appraisal can go wrong, so these can be borne in mind when preparing or improving the appraisal system. There are many things that can go wrong with appraisal. By reading this book you will be able to see what these are and, through careful design and implementation, create a system that does not go wrong. Appraisal fails at many levels. For example:

◆ provide conflicting messages to employees;

◆ a poor or inappropriate system;

◆ inadequate training of participants (both employees and managers);

◆ failure to implement the system properly;

◆ conflicting aims of the appraisal interview;

◆ failure to get people on board;

◆ takes too much time;

◆ takes too little time;

◆ poor follow up (eg providing promised training);

◆ no validation of the system.

This book will help you avoid these pitfalls. It does not provide a blueprint for any particular appraisal system, just the general rules which, if you follow them, will ensure you have an appraisal system acceptable to all and effective for the individual and for the organisation.

What do we need to watch out for?
In order to avoid a failing system, you should take account of some general points. In the first place, it should be remembered that the primary purpose of the appraisal system is not to improve individual perform-ance, though this is likely to be the end result, it is helping individual employees to successfully achieve what they want to achieve at work. Taking account of individual employees' aspirations and desires will have a beneficial effect on both the person and the organisa-tion. Take care over reducing individual anxieties about the system, ensure they know what the appraisal is for – there should be no hidden agendas.

The employee is also going to be concerned that the appraisal system is fair, integrated with other systems at work, and that they will receive equal treatment along with all other employees. If they know that certain people, or certain grades, obtain preferential treatment then they will resent the system and not be happy to take part. If that happens, then the system has failed.

The appraisal system has to consider staff development and training. Individual employees should have the opportunity to develop themselves, or be developed by the organisation. If the employee sees the appraisal simply as a way of checking performance, or having a general moan about the organisation with no personal benefits, then they will not take a full part in the system.

The organisation should take account of the need for autonomy and independence in individual employees. If an employee desires autonomy, then this should be considered in the appraisal. Can the appraisal be used to enhance autonomy? The individual should not think that the appraisal exists to 'bring them into line', to reduce their freedom of action in the job. This will only reduce performance.

Avoiding pitfalls

Another potential pitfall is that employees may be worried about biased or deliberately malicious appraisers. It is not uncommon for there to be a poor relationship between an employee and their line manager. In these cases the appraisal system must be designed to ensure that systematic bias does not occur, or that if it does, then the appraisee has a means of having this addressed. This might entail the use of an alternative appraiser.

The employee may also be concerned about the hidden agenda. As we will examine in the next chapter, there should be no hidden agenda if the organisation is truly open. No one benefits from a hidden agenda. They only exist so people can play politics, and playing politics is not acceptable in an organisation which wishes to treat employees fairly and which wishes to be productive.

When designing appraisal systems it is important to consider the position not only of the employees, but also of the managers who will not only be appraised, but will also be appraisers. There are a number of concerns often expressed by managers. Just like appraisees they will have a range of anxieties and concerns about the appraisal system, such as whether it will be effective, whether they have adequate training and experience to carry out appraisals, or whether they are aware of the training and development opportunities available within the organisation.

An appraisal system must be acceptable to both appraisees and appraisers. These considerations should always be in the forefront of your mind when you are designing the system. This is a very good reason why, during the process of design, you consult with potential participants and take their views into account.

THE STRUCTURE OF THE BOOK

The next chapter examines what is meant by the open organisation, and how it can work effectively for the employee and for the employer, and how it will help determine whether an appraisal system is going to work.

Chapter 3 is concerned with understanding the purpose of the appraisal, whether it is a simple performance review, or whether it is going to examine training and development needs, or long term career goals.

Chapter 4 is concerned with who should take on the role of appraiser, as this will vary from organisation to organisation. It also examines the issue of training the participants in the skills required for appraisal, such as negotiating and bargaining skills, counselling, skills and interviewing skills.

Chapter 5 examines how the job description and person specification are developed, and how they are used in the appraisal; eg ensuring that the person is fulfilling all aspects of the job, or examining how the job is changing over time because of the appraisee's specific skills or interests.

Chapter 6 focuses on the various kinds of appraisal that can be carried out. These include the type of appraisal normally carried out, where the supervisor or line manager appraises the individual, peer appraisal, team appraisal and upward appraisal.

Chapter 7 focuses on 360 degree appraisal, where information relevant to the appraisal is obtained from a number of sources, including the appraisee's managers and subordinates.

Chapter 8 focuses on practical aspects of preparing for the appraisal, the kinds of data that can be used in the appraisal interview, how they should be collected, and how all participants should prepare for the interview.

Chapter 9 examines the appraisal interview itself. When and where should the interview take place? What questions should be asked? How should the report be discussed and compiled?

Chapter 10 is concerned with how the appraisal should be followed up, and also examines ways of validating the system. There is little point in having a system that is glossy and expensive but does not work, and there is little point in proposing training that is not then conducted.

The final chapter looks at the present and future state of staff appraisal. What is its role in organisations? The book is about improving staff appraisal, so what should we see in the future? At the end of the book there is a guide to further information and a glossary of terms.

$$(2)$$

The open organisation and appraisal

In this chapter:

◆ **What is an open organisation?**

◆ **How the open organisation benefits the employer and the employee**

◆ **Appraisal and the open organisation**

◆ **Why do appraisals fail?**

THE OPEN ORGANISATION
Many larger organisations have well-designed staff appraisals, run by trained individuals who prepare appropriate paperwork and hold regular staff appraisal meetings with appraisees – yet the appraisal system still does not work. Why?

One of the main problems with such organisations lies in the organisation itself. Many organisations are very secretive about operations, about organisational accounts, about pay structures, negotiations with staff, performance-related pay, etc. Many staff can become demotivated by this, by not knowing how the organisation works.

There are differences between commercial organisations and public organisations. The current approach to many public organisations in the UK is to treat them as commercial institutions that are supposed to be run profitably. This is a major mistake. A university or a hospital cannot be run profitably, unless they are genuinely private. UK universities receive virtually all their money from the government: hospitals in the National Health Service likewise. They cannot be truly private, functioning for profit to distribute among shareholders. For these organisations openness is very important, it is crucial to the open society in which we are supposed to live.

Organisations, perhaps particularly public organisations, can tie themselves in bureaucratic knots in their human resource procedures, including appraisal. An organisation can end up being ineffective for most employees except higher managers. These managers make up the policies; they may even believe they are doing the right thing for the employees – but they do not consult with the workforce, so they may get it seriously wrong. Managers of certain kinds of organisations can be very blinkered in their approach to understanding the workforce. A paternalistic approach, where the worker is not consulted and the manager thinks they know best, is not appropriate.

This chapter takes a broad look at the open organisation and how it can work effectively for the employee and for the employer, and how it will help determine whether an appraisal system is going to work. The open organisation enables employees to have a say in the way the organisation works, because the management structure is flatter, policies and procedures are not cloaked in secrecy, and there is genuine consultation with the workforce which can have a serious impact on organisational policy.

Organisational openness

There is a trend in parts of society for greater openness. The British Government claims that it is increasing openness, that people have greater access to government records than ever before. Without getting into the debate about whether there really is more openness or not, many people believe that society will run more effectively if we have access to information. A closed society, one which runs secretly, where people live in fear and are told how to behave – in other words a fascist society – is considered by most of us to be a very poor kind of society to live in – so why do we put up with working in organisations which are essentially fascist?

The analogy is a good one. Organisations which are run in an open manner are considered to be healthier and better to work in than ones where procedures are kept secret from most employees. Employees working in secretive organisations are often more unhappy; less trusting of managers, and less motivated to work effectively than employees working in open organisations. Employees do not want to be told what to do more than is necessary.

People want to be trusted; they want to know that the people who employ them value them. In order for this to occur it is important that an organisation is open with regard to its procedures and policies, and that employees can become involved in decision-making (where appropriate).

WHAT IS OPENNESS?

◆ consultation;

◆ involvement in organisational decision-making;

◆ open policies and procedures;

- a flat management structure;

- having rights and responsibilities;

- recognition of the needs of the individual, not just in relation to work.

Openness is about ensuring the individual is involved in the organisation and the way it works. If people are involved they are more likely to be motivated. If they are motivated they will be happier and will work more effectively.

An open organisation has agreed objectives (what the organisation is for), scope (the activities it engages in) and principles (how it engages in activities, and limits to activities). An organisation should be egalitarian. Many organisations pay lip-service to openness, using terms such as autonomy, but not actually having procedures in place which will enable worker autonomy.

In terms of the individual the open organisation should allow people the freedom to control their own working practices as far as is practicable within the remit of the organisation. For instance, one of the main activities of a university lecturer is to lecture. The main constraints are going to be that the lecture must be delivered at a particular time and a particular place, and that any assessment relating to that lecture should be marked and processed by a particular date. How the lecturer designs the lecture, where they research and write it, where they do the marking, should be irrelevant to the organisation, as long as it does not impinge either on the lecturer's other duties, or the duties of other members of staff.

Models for openness

There are many models for the open organisation. Choosing or devising an appropriate one will depend on the type of organisation, the way it is currently run, and the members of the organisation. True openness is very difficult to achieve. There are many obstacles, from owners and managers to the workers themselves. Even if true openness is not achieved, it is important to try to implement some open procedures.

INFORMATION THAT SHOULD BE AVAILABLE

This will vary according to the size and the nature of the organisation. There are some things that should be readily available, such as organisational policies and procedures on employment (such as selection and recruitment, human resources management, staff appraisal), on company ethics and policies, on pay conditions, etc. An organisation should, where possible, also involve staff in decision-making. After all, the organisation is dependent on the staff so it should look to them regarding organisational matters such as company direction.

Richard Malter and Benjamin Geer (open-organizations.org) have proposed a series of processes and rules for the open organisation. The functional rules appropriate for large organisations which wish to develop openness include:

1. **Self-management.** As far as possible, individuals in a working group (eg department) should be free to discuss and decide among themselves how they are going to manage the work, rather than have it imposed from above.

2. **Best practice.** If a job is worth doing, it is worth doing well.

3. **Respect for skill.** Members of the organisation (including managers) should respect the skills of the workers. Staff expertise should be drawn on as appropriate for particular tasks. This has implications for teams. Team leaders should be aware of the strengths and weaknesses of the people in their team and, as much as possible, play to individual strengths.

4. **Public ownership of knowledge.** This is particularly important for public organisations.

5. **Diversity.** A range of approaches to solving problems can co-exist, without one hindering the others.
Diversity can increase the chances of success in
attaining goals and the discovery of new and better
working practices.

TRANSPARENCY AND OPENNESS

The term transparency is widely used to refer to
openness, to matters where employees should be as-
sured by the organisation that the organisation is
serving their best interests. Organisations should be
transparent in decision making and in reporting, for
instance, making all emails and the minutes of meetings
available in public folders. This makes the management
of the organisation accountable to staff. In publicly
funded organisations, these materials should (mostly)
be available to the general public, so making accountable to the people who fund that organisation. The
problem is that it is likely that there will be too much
information, so organisations should ensure there is
good indexing of information, and it should make sure
there are executive summaries available.

Too much openness?

In a large organisation, it is possible to be too open.
While it is a very good thing to consult with staff over
matters including the staff appraisal system, too much
consultation can interfere with the effectiveness of staff

to carry out their work. Openness does not mean providing all information to everyone all the time. Too much paperwork (or emailwork) will mean that staff become overburdened with consultation papers.

GOOD REASONS FOR SECRECY

There are good reasons why an organisation does not publicise all its activities. In the commercial world to disclose commercially-sensitive information may provide competitors with useful information which could end up reducing the profits of the organisation. It may be ethically inappropriate to disclose salaries of employees (with the exception of directors). It is inappropriate to have personal details of employees available for all to see.

Autonomy

Organisations should recognise the need for autonomy in individuals, departments and teams. Along with transparency, autonomy is the most important concept relating to the open organisation. A high level of autonomy is associated with the recognition that diverse working practices are acceptable and appropriate. People work differently, they have varying strengths and weaknesses, and different approaches to doing the job. As long as the outcome is consistent with the agreed objectives of the organisation then this diversity should be accepted. Such diversity ensures inclusivity for workers. Many organisations impose unnecessary limits to working practices, believing that they are ensuring staff are working towards the common organisational goal. This is erroneous. Restrictions are most likely to reduce performance through reducing autonomy. In other words, managers may impose a superficial collectivism.

ANXIETIES AND ISSUES ABOUT APPRAISAL AND THE OPEN ORGANISATION

People have a range of anxieties and concerns regarding staff appraisal. The open organisation will help reduce these concerns. People worry on a range of levels, about many things. The open organisation has to allow these anxieties to be aired. If an appraisal system is imposed without consultation then it will not be possible to air these concerns. At an early stage of development it is important to allow people the freedom to air their concerns and to have them dealt with. In this way they become more likely to accept the appraisal system. This section deals with some of the issues people might have.

The relationship between work role and self-development

Most employees are not entirely clear about the role they play in the organisation, the expectations of the organisation, and their own concerns about personal development. A good appraisal system in an open organisation will enable these issues to be addressed. As we shall see later in the book, the consideration of the various tasks carried out by the employee will help them see the context of their position within the organisation. Appraisal will link this to the individual's personal needs for development and growth, whether this is through training, or through enabling them to change their roles. The appraisal system will help the individual employee see the significance of their job. Understanding this will help the person value themselves within the organisation.

The problem with a poor appraisal system is that it may act as a barrier to personal growth and development. The appraisal system must take care to ensure that the relationship between life and work is fully considered. We do not achieve all our personal growth through work.

Motivation

Motivation is very difficult to measure. Motivation to work effectively, to be productive, is achieved through a range of activities, from paying the employee appropriately for the job, to saying 'well done', to enabling someone to take on new responsibilities. Motivation is about recognising individual needs. The appraisal system will play a major role in ensuring that an individual is well motivated.

Autonomy and teamworking

Individuals play different roles in organisations. Individuals also have different personalities, and it is important that these are recognised. Some *jobs* require high levels of autonomy; others require high levels of supervision. Some *people* require high levels of autonomy; others require high levels of supervision. Some people like to be allowed to get on with things on their own; others prefer to work closely with others.

There is a tendency in many organisations to assume that we all work in 'teams', even when there is no formal team as such. A department is not a team. It might be, but do not make the mistake of assuming it is or should be. Some people do not work well in teams. A good appraisal system will recognise the differences between people and not assume that they are all alike. A good manager will recognise the differences between people, including those who are not good in teams. They will play to the strengths and cover the weaknesses of the members of the department.

People who like their independence at work will want to ensure that they have the opportunity to maximise and protect their own space and independence, and enable them to achieve personal growth on this basis. An appraisal system should be supportive of a person's independence and autonomy; it should not constrain and diminish it. That will only have the effect of demotivating the individual and reducing their effectiveness.

Bias and incompetence in the appraiser

The problem with appraisals is that they are carried out by people. The problem with people is that they are not always good at their tasks; they are sometimes biased or prejudiced against particular people. Appraisers are often the employee's line manager, and as we all know there are sometimes problems in the relationship between the line manager and the employee.

An appraisee might justifiably feel that they are not going to be fairly treated in the appraisal because they do not have a good relationship with the appraiser. This may be particularly difficult if the appraisal is concerned with providing rewards for performance, or providing suitable training for development, or for finding out who should have promotion. There are particular problems if the 360 degree appraisal system is implemented. In fact, the 360 degree appraisal should not be implemented if the organisation is not open. In any organisation there are friendships, alliances, enemies and malicious gossip. All may affect how any particular employee is rated. A truly open organisation will have fewer problems with this; but in the end people are people. The system must account for these problems.

Procedures to meet problems

A good appraisal will take account of both the legal and ethical issues involved here. An appraisal must not be discriminative. The appraisal system must have procedures in place for ensuring that discrimination does not take place; or, if there are particular problems, there are procedures for the employee to obtain redress for problems.

All participants in the appraisals should receive equal and fair treatment. If employees are convinced that the system will ensure this, then they will have more faith in the system and in the organisation. The problem arises if the employee thinks that the appraisal system subtly (or not so subtly) treats people in different roles differently within the system.

Incompetence in an appraiser is unacceptable. The appraisal system must include providing good training for people who are carrying out appraisals. An incompetently carried out appraisal is worse than no appraisal at all, and participants will cease to have faith in either the system or the organisation.

Performance, promotion and pay

Many people worry when the appraisal system is linked closely with pay-related performance issues. In many jobs, there are close links between performance and pay, and if this is the case then the appraisal system must ensure that measures of performance are valid, and that other purposes of appraisal (eg training and development) do not get mixed up with the assessment of performance.

Performance-related pay (PRP) is appropriate in organisations where performance can be operationalised and can be linked to individual or group performance. It is not appropriate where performance cannot be appropriately operationalised. Unfortunately, many organisations do not think like this. PRP for managers may not be appropriate as their performance cannot be linked directly to, for instance, organisational performance. In the end, it is usually the worker who produces, not the manager; so PRP may be more appropriate for workers than managers. Most managers will probably not like this view, but most workers do not like managers getting PRP when it is the workers who do the work. Managers only manage.

A further argument against PRP is that performance does not usually depend on the individual, but that the overall performance of the organisation depends on overall performance and other factors beyond the individual. For this reason, organisations should consider whether there should be any association between performance and pay.

PRP is a difficult issue, We all want more pay when we do well, but the system must be fair.

The hidden agenda

Procedures in an open organisation should not have a hidden agenda. The purposes of the appraisal should be open and clear at all stages. Individual employees in many organisations are often very cynical, and assume that managers and employers always have hidden agendas. Appraisals may be perceived as a means of establishing and keeping control of the workers. Perhaps this area is the most important when discussing the open organisation. An open organisation will not have hidden agendas, and employees will be less likely to believe that such hidden agendas exist.

Constant change

Many organisations tend to follow fashions; they pick up procedures from consultants and books, the latest trend in management thinking. Constant change can have a seriously detrimental effect on staff morale. If a new appraisal system is introduced, staff need to know that the system will be given a chance to work, and that another system will not be implemented the following year. People like continuity. It is important that the organisation gets it right, and then gives it time to work. Constantly changing procedures creates a lot of extra work for everyone. The introduction of a new appraisal system is inevitably going to be greeted negatively, unless the organisation works hard to show why the system is needed.

If managers buy into new fashions in business, they expect employees to buy into them as well. This is not always reasonable or acceptable. Employees want to get on with the job, and not be interfered with unnecessarily. They do not want new ideas every few months. Organisations do substantially change every now and again; they develop a new strategic direction, perhaps because they have new leaders, perhaps because the market is changing. If the organisation does change then the appraisal system can be used to help people come to terms with the change, perhaps through providing training for changes in job roles. If customary working practices have to be changed, it is important that the organisation enables employees to change. Beware though of innovation, a much maligned word, overused and dangerous. Sometimes traditional practice is the most appropriate. Do not institute change for change's sake.

What do employers want to find out?

Employees might worry that management is using the appraisal system to find out personal details about them, which might have implications for their job. For instance, are younger women thinking of having children? While it is illegal for employers to discriminate on the basis of whether a woman might later have children, it is not unknown. An open organisation with an open appraisal system should not experience a problem with this.

On the other hand, it is entirely appropriate for the organisation to want to find out about the workforce, how they are getting on at work, whether they are satisfied and if not why not, their ambitions and desires. This will help the organisation match individual and organisational needs. It will help identify people for promotion and transfer, and in the end aid productivity.

COMMITMENT

Commitment is critical: commitment from employees and from managers. Without this, the appraisal system will not be successful. Commitment can only arise when there is trust, honesty, and fairness in an organisation; and these only arise when the organisation is committed to openness. Commitment will only arise if there are adequate resources and training provided for participants, and if the organisation consults with staff at all stages of the development of the appraisal.

SO WHY DO APPRAISALS FAIL?

Following on from Chapter One, before we can show how appraisals can succeed, we should be aware of how they might fail. It is understandable that readers of this book might have negative views about appraisal, particularly if the systems they have dealt with in the past have been less than perfect. Once we identify the factors for failure, we can address them and help ensure appraisal will succeed.

Appraisal is almost ubiquitous in organisations, but as we have seen, it often fails both the employee and the employer. It is, in many cases, not good value for money. Appraisals in traditional organisations often give conflicting messages between encouragement and control: is the organisation trying to encourage workers or is it just trying to control their behaviour? In many cases, the employee believes the latter, even where the employer is genuinely trying to encourage. The problem is that the employer's encouragement is the employee's control. The employer is setting the agenda for work; the employee is expected to follow that agenda.

Creating win-win situations

Some organisations have shown that there are alternatives. Some organisations use both mangers and workers to set up systems, whereby every operation at work has an associated measure which is designed by, and therefore accepted by, both worker and manager. These measures then provide feedback to both worker and manager. If something goes wrong – and this is the key point – then it is the system that is in error, not the worker. This is fundamentally different to the way most organisations work, where control is considered key, even when it is implicit; even when the organisation genuinely believes it is not controlling.

If an appraisal system is going to work, then it must move away from notions of control, and be seen as a means whereby both the organisation and the worker have benefits, the win-win situation. In order for this to happen, the organisation must be open, and it should have systems in place which recognise that performance is not just about individuals, it is about the systems that are in place, it is about the way the organisation is structured and managed, and it is about recognising that workers are human beings.

CONCLUDING COMMENTS

The open organisation is conducive to worker satisfaction and individual and organisational effectiveness and performance. Having an open organisation, where workers have a genuine say in what happens in the organisation, where they are consulted over major decisions, where they are able to comment on their managers' performance, will underpin the partnership between the employee and the organisation, and an organisation with a reputation for caring about its workers, respecting their abilities, their skills, their differences, is more likely to attract more skilful, more able and more highly educated employees.

The purposes of appraisal

In this chapter:

◆ **Examining the purposes of appraisal**

◆ **Not just performance review**

◆ **Training and development**

◆ **Promotion and transfer**

◆ **Personal health**

◆ **Team development**

◆ **Job design**

◆ **Integrating objectives**

THE VARIOUS PURPOSES

Appraisals have a number of purposes, ranging from the performance review through training, to assessing the longer-term career development aspirations of the employee. It may involve assessing training and development needs, exploring the changing nature of the job, examining aspects of the job that might be creating difficulties; or aspects that are dull. An appraisal should never just involve a performance review. While this is valuable to the organisation, it does not consider the needs of the individual.

Organisations should not consider performance review to be the main purpose of appraisal. Performance arises out of a range of factors, and can be enhanced without even direct consideration of past and potential future performance. An appraisal can explicitly focus on, for instance, personal growth and team development, and once these are addressed properly performance will almost certainly be enhanced. Positive motivators work better than negative motivators.

Appraisal, then, can have a number of purposes, from the global need to increase the overall efficiency and effectiveness of the organisation, through an examination of the performance of individuals and teams, to a consideration of the needs of the individual, both within and beyond the organisation, ie training and development to improve job performance and satisfaction, and *an examination of the individual needs of the employee as a person – not just an employee.*

The appraisal system must ensure good practice is maintained throughout its implementation.

TIMING

The appraisal must be timed appropriately. Many organisations have fluctuating workloads. Some periods are more busy than others. If possible, it makes sense to organise appraisals to occur when the employee is less busy. If someone is in the busiest time of the year they are not going to want to prepare for and go through appraisal. While an appraisal system may outline the period or timings of the appraisal (eg one year, six months), this will have to be flexible depending on individual circumstances.

MOTIVATION

The appraisal can make or break the motivation of an employee. It can, in the space of an hour or two, motivate an unmotivated employee, or demotivate a highly motivated employee. As motivation has a strong correlation with productivity it is in the interests of the employer to try to avoid demotivating the employee. At worst, the appraisal can be presented in the style of a school report card ('could do better') – perhaps not the best of approaches.

Appraisal is a very useful outlet for employees to talk about themselves and their needs. It can be difficult in many organisations to find an opening to discuss one's own needs with the line manager or employer, yet managers and employers benefit from understanding the personal needs of the employee. In that way they can begin to understand not only the training someone might need to do their job more effectively, but what motivates different individuals. It is about establishing a relationship between the employee and the organisation which genuinely recognises the needs and individuality of the employee. If employees can achieve personal growth partly through the medium of the appraisal, then there will be positive organisational growth.

Appraisal is not only about reflection on past performance, it is also about considering the future, examining goals, ambitions and plans. It should not just be a linear process of exploring performance, looking at strengths and weaknesses, and providing objective plans for the next year, it should allow the employee the opportunity to discuss the future more widely, to explore what they hope to do in the longer term. Even when these ideas are very vague, it is helpful to discuss them with the appraiser, perhaps to give them some direction, and to give the appraiser food for thought.

APPRAISAL IS FOR THE EMPLOYER AS WELL AS THE EMPLOYEE

Appraisal is for the appraiser as well as the appraisee. The appraiser will, through the process of talking to employees substantively, learn a lot about both the workforce and the way the organisation is perceived. They must take these views seriously. It is a useful means by which to consider changes in the way the organisation is run.

The feedback the employer obtains from the appraisal process is very helpful in a changing environment. The context of the organisation in wider society is important, and the employer must understand what things change, and what things remain the same (there is a current focus on the need for constant innovation, which can be to the detriment of effective traditional procedures). Employees do understand a lot about the context of the organisation in society at large. Employers are wise to heed this knowledge.

PERFORMANCE REVIEW

Inevitably appraisal will be about performance. It is essential to understand where an employee is achieving well and where they are not as successful. It is just as essential to understand why. If an employee is achieving well in aspects of the job and not in others then understanding why is the first step to improving the situation. There are particular training and development needs which are not allowing the employee to perform to their potential. The job may be changing and the employee has not changed with it. The employee may be demotivated for other reasons. Whatever the problem, the appraisal is a good place to explore solutions.

The setting of objectives should be a careful process that takes into account a number of factors, including:

- performance regarding previous objectives;

- aptitude at job;

- personal circumstances;

- future potential;

- the changing work environment.

Reasonable objectives give employees sensible guidelines against which to work for the coming year. If these guidelines are not present, or are not sufficiently clear, employees may not know what is expected of them.

Performance criteria

These should be chosen carefully; especially for situations where performance is not easily quantifiable (that is the case for many white collar jobs). There is little point in setting objectives which are not measurable in terms of actual performance. For some jobs, quantifiable assessment is easy, for others it is more difficult, if not impossible. Any system of objective setting must be rational and fair, allow systematic measurement, and be stable over time so that employees are not constantly being subjected to change – for the sake of change. Stability enables the organisation to monitor individual and organisational trends.

Possible quantifiable measures include:

◆ direct financial indices, such as sales volume or profit;

◆ direct quantifiable measures, such as units of production or number of customers;

◆ ratios, such as errors per 100 transactions or sales per 100 contacts;

◆ time factors, such as the time it takes to complete a task, or success at meeting deadlines;

- judgemental scales, such as supervisor ratings or peer ratings.

Performance is never just about the individual, it involves the systems in which the individual works, the people they work with, and people they come into contact with outside work. Beware of simplistic measures. They can easily be construed as unfair, which may have legal implications. Objectives should be used within the appraisal interview as items of discussion, rather than the means of using a stick to beat the employee. If an objective has not been met then it is the purpose of the appraisal interview to explore the reasons why, not just to assume that the employee is incompetent or lazy.

Objectives of performance review

A performance review should be carried out regularly, with clear objectives, which are, at least in part, devised by or with the individual employee – this is essential to performance management. As far as possible or practical, let employees determine their own objectives. This is a laudable idea, as long as the organisation is helping the individual achieve their personal goals in life and work. It is entirely reasonable for an employee to ask, 'what's in it for me?' That is not selfish or greedy. If the employer wants the best performance out of an individual then they must be prepared to support that individual towards achieving their own personal goals.

In a good open organisation, performance management is an attempt to move towards allowing the individual a say in designing and implementing their own performance targets and goals. It is a move away from traditional command and control organisational structure towards a facilitation model of leadership.

Performance-related pay (PRP)

An appraisal system is often used to determine levels of PRP, though there are inherent dangers in such systems. If PRP does not apply to all members of an organisation then those outside the system (usually non-managers) are likely to be resentful. While many managers will not like this recommendation, PRP should never be used unless it is an objective system and it is fair to all employees. PRP should never be applied only to managers.

Praise, recognition and criticism

The appraiser is in a useful position to provide praise, recognition and criticism. We are all familiar with the benefits of praise, or recognising a job well done, which in turn leads the individual to feel valued by the organisation, which in turn leads to a motivated workforce and a happy organisation. Unfortunately, as discussed elsewhere, some managers find it difficult to provide praise and recognition for a job well done.

Constructive criticism is also important. If an individual's performance has been poor for some reason then, once the reasons for this performance are established, it is appropriate to provide constructive criticism. If it is not constructive, criticism will be demotivating, which will only exacerbate the problem.

TRAINING AND DEVELOPMENT

One of the main purposes of appraisal is to ascertain training needs and ensure these needs are met. The modern world requires effective staff development and training. Keeping up is very difficult, particularly in cutting edge industries such as computing, but also in every industry experiencing change – particularly where there is a constant flow of employees. The loss of a job for life has its costs, including providing training and development for new or inexperienced employees. Even small businesses making traditional crafts have to keep up with health and safety regulations, other legal issues, demographic changes and market trends.

In order to do this the organisation must provide training for employees; and often, the employee is the best person to ask to help ascertain such needs. The appraisal is the ideal forum for this.

Employees should have access to any training courses that will help them in their job and for their career development. The appraisal can help determine training needs in a number of ways, such as by:

◆ asking the appraisee what they need (in relation to both current needs and future hopes and aspirations);

◆ asking their colleagues and supervisor;

◆ assessing problems with performance and discussing how these may be rectified;

◆ looking at the appraisee's history of training and seeing how that can be built on.

Assessing needs
There is little advantage in sending employees on training courses without accurately assessing their particular needs. Individuals and jobs differ so much that while off-the-peg training courses are useful in many circumstances they may sometimes be a waste of resources, and it may be necessary to design appropriate training programmes.

It is often the case that performance is less than perfect not because the employee is incompetent or lazy but because they do not have the requisite skills for particular tasks. For example, an employee has been given the task of negotiating to purchase some goods. In other buying situations they may have performed well, but in a novel situation, faced with trained and experienced negotiators they are out of their depth. Without analysing the situation, you may decide to withhold the person's bonus because they have not succeeded in obtaining the right price for the goods; but if you assess their needs then you may discover that the person needs training in basic negotiating skills.

PROMOTION AND TRANSFER

Promotion and transfer are separate but linked purposes of staff appraisals. This kind of appraisal is used not only to assess an individual's effectiveness in their current job, but also to try to predict how well they would perform in a different role. If the role is very different then, as in job selection, a great deal of care needs to be taken when judging potential effectiveness. Do not assume that because someone is good in one role they will be good in another. The new role may well involve very different tasks and perhaps more responsibility.

The danger of promoting someone too high, to their level of incompetence, is called the 'Peter Principle'. If this occurs, neither the organisation nor the individual will benefit. It is likely that the organisation will lose money by having an incompetent person in a particular position, and the individual will be dissatisfied trying to do a job for which they are not well suited – not to mention the demotivating effects an incompetent manager can have on staff (we can all think of examples).

ASSESSING POTENTIAL

Assessing potential is similar to, but not the same as appraisal for promotion or transfer, where there is a specific vacancy available and the organisation is looking for someone to fill it. Here the purpose is to find out which employees are likely to rise through the ranks, and providing them with appropriate training and guidance.

It benefits the organisation and the individual to find out who may be a 'high flyer', keep an eye on their development, and provide suitable training and preparation for their future roles. If a person seems suitable for higher management, then they can be placed on a programme of courses designed to prepare them for that kind of role. Accurate assessment is crucial in these cases because training is often very expensive; if the wrong individual is chosen the organisation may waste a lot of money. Remember the Peter Principle.

Likewise, if someone appears to be more suited to a different type of job within the organisation, perhaps a transfer to a different department, they should be prepared for that. This may again involve training, or perhaps arranging a temporary transfer to see how they get on.

Making an appraisal

In these cases, it is important to collect relevant data. It is helpful to interview the people the employee works with, to interview colleagues, supervisors and subordinates, to create a general picture of the work the employee carries out, the problems inherent in the job, their strengths and weaknesses, and to obtain detailed information about the job to which they may be transferred; in order that time can be spent with the employee determining whether the transfer or promotion is feasible or appropriate.

Using these findings as a basis for discussion, the appraisal can then be used to draw out further information to complete the picture, and to determine the best direction for the employee's career. This type of appraisal also decreases the risk of possible future job dissatisfaction. Personal information obtained from this process can also help determine training needs.

VOCATIONAL GUIDANCE

This is linked to development. There is a range of situations where vocational guidance is necessary. It might occur when the individual is being considered for a move within the organisation, and it should also be considered when the individual is being made redundant. For the latter case, the organisation is morally responsible to provide help for individuals who are losing their jobs. It could be argued that this is not strictly staff appraisal, but it is linked. Appraisal is about ensuring the right person is in the right job, to maximise job satisfaction and productivity, so providing vocational advice is crucial.

A range of techniques are used in vocational guidance, particularly questionnaires and psychological tests. These provide detailed information about the individual, including aptitudes, personality and interests. The analysis of psychological measures will help generate ideas for careers and career changes. The findings can be explained to the employee, suggesting potentially suitable jobs, and providing the means of obtaining further information.

The organisation should also ensure that the redundant worker has all the necessary skills for obtaining another job, such as:

- writing a curriculum vitae;

- completing application forms;

- interview techniques.

By providing this service, the organisation goes some way to ensuring the leaving employee has a reasonable chance of obtaining another job.

PERSONAL HEALTH

We live in a rapidly changing society, in which some claim that we are active 24 hours a day, seven days a week (but just try to find an ordinary shop open at 6 or 7 a.m.). We are expected to work longer hours (contradicting EU regulations), go shopping in the middle of the night, and run our lives without sleep – or so the zeitgeist informs us. Of course this is nonsense. A sensible organisation will ensure that its employees do not work long, irregular hours as this is not conducive to productivity. It is well known that organisations on the Continent, where people work shorter hours, have higher productivity. There is plenty of evidence that it is better to work a good six hour day than a poor ten hour day.

Two key areas regarding mental health are stress and the work-home relationship. Both are related, and both have a major impact on the individual and the organisation. If a person works too long in an environment that is not conducive to health, then it is likely they will be away from work because of stress-related problems. Similarly, if the person cannot balance the work-home relationship, usually because the organisation is being difficult, then there can be problems.

The work-home balance

The government has recognised the importance of balancing the work-home relationship. Our family and personal relationships can be damaged because we work too long, or because we work irregular hours or shifts. A good organisation will consider the work-home balance through the appraisal system. There is a wide range of flexible working options. These include:

- part-time working;

- flexible hours;

- flexi-time (over a week, a month, or a year);

- providing leave, paid or unpaid, to care for children or aging relatives;

- working from home.

Stress is recognised as a major problem for individuals and for the economy. Up to 15 million working days a year are lost through stress. An organisation must ensure that the appraisal system provides an outlet for people to discuss stress-related matters. This can only be done effectively in an open and trusting organisation, where the appraisee feels confident that any health-related information will not be used against them. In larger organisations, occupational health departments can make a valuable contribution.

TEAM DEVELOPMENT

In organisations where the team is important – and it is a concept that can be over-rated – the appraisal is the place to consider team development. Teams are not always important in an organisation; sometimes the individual is more important. For instance, in higher education, lecturers are selected on the basis that they are *not* good team players. The qualification required, the PhD, requires that the individual is good at working alone, meeting challenges alone, and dealing with problems alone. This is why managing academics is often seen as trying to train a team of cats to pull a cart. Other organisations use similar kinds of individuals, so it is important not to see teams as critical at all times.

But, in many organisations the team plays a critical role. How individuals function together can impact on the success or otherwise of the organisation. If people cannot work together then that may be conducive to a poor atmosphere in the workplace and hence social problems, let alone the impact on productivity because of the failure to work together.

The appraiser has a role in trying to ensure any problems within the team are resolved. One good way is through the 360 appraisal, discussed in detail in Chapter Seven. In this form of appraisal, the appraiser collects information about the appraisee, not only from line managers, but also from colleagues and subordinates. This is an excellent way to explore team-related issues, though it needs care when analysing the data from such an appraisal to ensure that individuals are not being maligned unfairly by colleagues, perhaps because of some non-work-related axe that someone is grinding.

Team building is a difficult exercise, and the appraiser should treat it cautiously, remembering that it is important to understand the broader perspective, not just take the word of a couple of individuals who may have their own personal issues.

JOB REDESIGN

Appraisals can also serve important organisational functions. Sometimes the organisation needs to review the *job*, not just the person. Jobs are often badly structured (see Chapter 5 for information about creating a job description), many jobs being a hotch-potch of tasks, thrown together to serve a particular purpose at a particular time and built up over the years by people taking on various tasks at different times. If the personnel department tried to analyse this kind of job they would not find any coherence. There would be no rational reason why these miscellaneous tasks should be put together to be carried out by one person under a single job title; nor why two people ostensibly with the same job title are doing very different jobs.

When the organisation has jobs like this, it is useful to ask people, within the appraisal, for their views on whether the job is effective as it is, or whether it might be redesigned in a more coherent way. The organisation may find that one of these apparently chaotic jobs is being carried out by a person who is perfectly happy with that range of tasks, in which case it may be best to let them get on with it (do not over-manage, things do not need changing for the sake of change). On the other hand, a person might be less than fully productive precisely because their job – not the person – is inefficient. They may be dissatisfied with their job because they are not clear about why they need to carry out certain roles.

INTEGRATING OBJECTIVES

The various purposes of appraisal are often closely linked within a single appraisal interview. They are not intended to be separate, they should flow together seamlessly. Appraisals will rightly consider more than one of the above categories. For instance, if you are carrying out an appraisal for the purposes of performance review, you are likely to include an assessment of training needs, future potential, and the setting of objectives. They are all part of a single package.

It can be difficult to review performance with a view to providing reward at the same time as assessing individual needs and personal issues. An appraisee is unlikely to be entirely honest if there is reward at stake!

Having multiple purposes does not mean all the above have to be included. Each appraisal interview should be carefully designed, and its purposes clearly agreed between both parties. Appraisals may be carried out outside of the regular system because of specific purposes, such as promotion and transfer, or because a specific issue has arisen. Do not treat appraisal as a once a year chore, but as continual activity.

ADDRESSING PROBLEM AREAS

If any performance-related rewards are assigned separately from the rest of the appraisal, then the employee can be more open with the appraiser about personal and professional issues, and develop a better sense of trust. If the appraisee believes that you are forming subjective judgements on the basis of comments in the appraisal interview, and that you have the power to withhold bonuses, then trust can be hard to establish and the appraisee will not state their viewpoints openly.

This problem is difficult to resolve. In some cases it may be possible to set up objective criteria for the award of bonuses. In others it is not. If objective and fair criteria are available, then there is no reason why rewards should not be linked to the appraisal. If not, then they *should not be linked* because the appraisee would not jeopardise the chance of obtaining a bonus by, for example, criticising the way the organisation is run if the appraiser is the boss!

Even the best appraisal systems are, like anything involving people, open to abuse. For example, the appraiser may try to set objectives that the appraisee believes are too high, or the data used in the interview may be perceived as inaccurate or biased. A good appraisal system gets round this by having grievance procedures and arbitration where appraisees can approach other authorities if they believe they have been treated unfairly. Of course, formal appeals systems should only be used when all informal means have been tried. There is no gain in making disagreements formal unless absolutely necessary; such procedures can be expensive, time-consuming, and can lead to anger and bitterness between employee and manager; and that is something to be avoided wherever possible.

CASE STUDY

Jack finds a better strategy

Sam is being appraised by Jack. They have already examined various aspects of Sam's performance over the last six months when Jack says:

'I'd like to turn to this problem you're having with stock levels. I hear that levels are so low you're having difficulty meeting orders on time, and that the Whitesons order was two days late. You need to make sure levels are adequate at all times. You can't afford to be late with these orders.'

'Yes, but the problem is . . .'

Jack interrupts: 'I don't want to hear why, I just want it sorted out – quickly.'

Clearly this approach is problematic. A better approach would be:

'I'd like to turn to this problem you're having with stock levels. I hear that levels are so low you're having difficulty meeting orders on time, and one order was late. Can you tell me about it?'

Sam: 'Yes, it's true I'm afraid. Stock levels had been kept down because we had been having problems with high levels. If you recall, we discussed this a few months ago and agreed to decrease levels. Now we have all these extra orders production are having difficulty keeping up.'

Jack: 'Yes, I see what you mean. What do you think we should do about it?'

Sam: 'Well, we're over the worst of it now, stock levels are rising again, and I think we can get our orders out on schedule. But for the future, if we had more information from marketing I don't think the problem would have arisen. We just weren't prepared for the extra orders.'

Jack: 'Ok, I'll get onto marketing and make sure you get the information you need. I suppose monthly would be all right?'

Sam: 'Yes.'

Jack: 'What about future stock levels?'

Sam: 'If I get the right information from marketing then we can keep them down to our previously agreed figure.'

Jack: 'Right, we'll give it a try and review the situation in six months.'

Comment

You can see the difference between the two strategies. In the first Sam is not given a chance to put across his position. He is simply blamed for what had gone wrong and told to put it right. This strategy may well lead to resentment and hostility. The second dialogue is much better. Here, Jack draws the information out of Sam by asking open questions, 'Can you tell me about it?' and then asks Sam for his own solution: 'What do you think we should do about it?' The problem is presented, the solution is found by the employee, and appropriate action is planned, including following up six months later.

Also, Jack uses 'you' in the first dialogue. This isolates Sam from the organisation, suggests the problem is entirely his and that he alone has to find the solution. In the second dialogue 'you' becomes 'we', the problem becomes an organisation problem, and the organisation will work together with Sam to find the solution. The use of 'we' in this context is less likely to alienate the appraisee and thus less likely to create resentment against the organisation.

$$\overset{\displaystyle\bigodot}{}$$

$$\text{4}$$

People and appraisal skills

In this chapter:

- ◆ **Who should conduct staff appraisals?**

- ◆ **Appraisal skills, eg interview techniques, listening, counselling skills, negotiation, job analysis**

This chapter is concerned with the role of appraiser and the skills involved in appraisal (both for the appraiser and the appraisee). The person who conducts the appraisal will vary from organisation to organisation. In smaller organisations, it will be the boss who appraises everyone. In larger organisations the appraisal system may cascade down from the top. In many cases the appraiser will be the line manager. This chapter will examine the issue of training the participants in the skills required for appraisal, negotiating and bargaining skills, counselling skills, interviewing skills, and giving and receiving feedback. There are also legal issues relating to the appraisal, ranging from ensuring ethical and fair treatment of participants, through to health and safety issues, and organisational policy on matters such as the work-home balance and stress. The appraiser must be aware of these issues.

The appraiser should have a detailed knowledge and understanding of the appraisee's work, they should have a detailed understanding of the requirements of their department and of the organisation as a whole, and, importantly, they should have the authority to make resources available, or to determine whether they are available, to ensure that agreed objectives and targets can be met. If targets are set which require training and the training is not forthcoming, then the appraisee will have little faith in the system and it will become a paper exercise.

WHO SHOULD CONDUCT STAFF APPRAISALS?

The appraisal can be carried out by a number of people, for instance:

- the line manager;

- supervisor;

- employer;

- colleague;

- human resources manager;

◆ a specially trained appraisal officer.

Which person is actually used will depend on the size and structure of the organisation, and on who is being appraised. There are valid arguments for all these individuals to be the appraiser, and equally valid arguments against them.

For instance, it is desirable that the employer should conduct appraisals, because that is the person who should be most aware of the needs and performance of all employees, but in organisations that are larger than about 20 people, this is probably impractical. The immediate supervisor or line manager is a good choice, because that is the person to whom the employee is immediately responsible. The problem might be that the employee may not have a good relationship with that person. If this is the case then this relationship may well be an issue that the appraisee wishes to raise in the interview. A specially trained appraisal officer from the human resources department may have a broad knowledge of the appraisal system and of the organisation itself, but they may have little direct knowledge of the job the appraisee does.

These arguments can be extended indefinitely. This book cannot provide all the answers, what is provided is a set of guidelines for potential appraisers to make appropriate decisions *for their organisation* about who should appraise whom.

Who appraises whom

In the majority of cases the supervisor or line manager conducts the appraisal. This person will have a good knowledge of both the job and the person. If there is a good professional relationship between the two people the appraisal can be very effective. The appraiser will be in a position to comment effectively and with knowledge about the appraisec's performance, and probably about the appraisee's personal training and development needs. It is quite likely that in the past the supervisor or line manager has done the appraisee's job. If the work is particularly specialist, then the line manager may be the only person in the organisation who is qualified to comment effectively on perform-ance. Performance is not always objectively measur-able and quantifiable. If this is the case the appraiser should be someone who is knowledgeable about the job.

Sometimes the best argument against the line manager or supervisor carrying out the appraisal is their close working relationship. Whether this is because there is a good personal relationship, or because they work together and so the appraisee does not wish to discuss some issues openly, this can create difficulties with the appraisal. In both cases issues that should be discussed openly in the appraisal may not be brought out.

Can the appraisee talk freely?

If there is a difficult working relationship then the discussion of certain issues may be either taboo or, if discussed, lead to an even worse working relationship. If the appraisee wishes to criticise the way they are managed or supervised, the place to discuss this is the appraisal. It is difficult for one to criticise the person one is talking to. It is not reasonable to ask the appraisee to make such open criticism. There has to be other avenues for expression, hence flexibility in the appraisal system.

There are other reasons why the line manager or supervisor should not be used. The performance of the appraisee may have been adversely affected by their relationship with the supervisor. What if the supervisor does not respect or acknowledge the appraisee's performance? They may be prejudiced. How can the appraisee tell the supervisor that their performance is poor because of the way the supervisor treats them? It may be that the appraisee lacks motivation because the supervisor does not provide appropriate praise and encouragement for their work. It is unlikely this can be discussed openly.

During the appraisal it is important that the appraisee can talk to someone freely about whatever problems they feel exist. Where possible, the appraisee should have some influence on who acts as their appraiser.

Cascade

A good appraisal system in a large organisation can work well using a cascading system, whereby the top managers appraise the middle managers and so on. This ensures that everyone is involved in the system, and will lead to cohesiveness. This does not mean that it is always a 'superior' carrying out the appraisal; in many organisations peers will carry out the appraisals. In these cases, issues relating to the provision of reward and training and development programmes are important, because it is not usual for peers to provide this.

APPRAISAL SKILLS

Both the appraiser and the appraisee should have a range of skills in order to make the best of the appraisal. An appraisal should not involve going round in circles and not getting anywhere. During the appraisal interview it is important to be honest and direct. You need to get at the issues that matter, so while you should be tactful, you should ensure you get to the point. Be direct, be clear. Having said that, you should ensure that the approach is conversational, not heavy-handed; and you do need to be sensitive. If possible the appraisal should be fun! You might want to consider where to carry out the appraisal. If the office is seen as the 'boss's room' then perhaps you should carry it out elsewhere – as long as the venue is private.

Preparation

This is critical to the success of the appraisal, and we explore this in detail later in the book. You will need to ensure that you have collected the right data before conducting the appraisal. Both parties need to consider what subjects need to be addressed during the interview, and both need to be prepared for what the other wants to say. There should be no surprises during the interview. Because the appraisal may be about making important decisions, it is crucial that adequate preparation is carried out to ensure that the decisions that are made are the right ones. Without preparation the appraisal will be useless.

Encouragement

As discussed elsewhere, staff should be encouraged to take an active interest in the appraisal system through a recognition that it is of benefit to all members of staff. This is best achieved through a training process.

Praise

It should not have to be stated that people are motivated by praise. Unfortunately, in many organisations this is not recognised. Managers sometimes believe that they can achieve results through bullying, shouting and harassing. This attitude is not limited to unreconstructed old-fashioned industry but permeates through many of our workplaces. In some industries, managers are promoted from the rank and file, and when they achieve promotion, they find that they just cannot cope; so instead of managing effectively, they manage through bullying.

One of the key skills in an appraisal system is praise and encouragement. Money is not the main motivator for performance; for many people, praise is far more effective. A well-chosen word in the right place can perform miracles. While this should take place throughout the year, appraisal is a good place to ensure that praise is given.

INTERVIEWING SKILLS

You are trying to obtain information from the appraisee, consider that information, and then find appropriate means of addressing what is being said. These are interviewing skills. Some appraisees are reluctant to talk, or at least to talk about what is important. You need to be able to draw the information out of the appraisee. You need to be able to praise good work, and be constructively critical when the work is not up to an appropriate standard. You need to be able to negotiate with the individual how they are going to improve, their training requirements, what their problems are.

There are many kinds of interview, but certain rules apply across all kinds of interviewing, including appraisal. Interviewing is a *communication skill*. Before an effective interview can take place, both parties need to know what the other expects. If both agree what the interview is going to be about, it is more likely to succeed. If not, then neither will really be listening to what the other has to say. Since they are expecting different things, they will hear different things. Suppose you are only interested in reviewing the performance of the appraisee and setting new objectives for the coming year, but they wish to discuss problems they are having relating to co-workers. You may find yourselves talking at cross-purposes and achieve little except mutual dissatisfaction. Both before and during the appraisal, each party has to *listen* to the other.

LISTENING SKILLS

It is important for both parties in the appraisal to engage in *active listening*. This is crucial to a good interview, and to effective communication. Both parties should show the other that they are being listened to properly, not simply heard, but concentrating on what is being said and not losing interest. The basic rules are:

- do not make hasty judgements;

- do not listen selectively;

- do not interrupt;

- feed back information to ensure it has been heard properly (see below).

The appraiser who makes hasty judgements without hearing all sides of an argument is ineffective. If you do not listen to all the appraisee has to say then you may miss something of value. Likewise for the appraiser who listens selectively. If you have decided before the interview what your conclusions will be, and only hear what you want to hear, then why have the appraisal at all?

Apart from being rude, constant interruptions can upset the flow of the appraisee's argument. They can appear aggressive. Interruptions are justified when the appraisee (or the appraiser for that matter) is rambling, or if the other party does not understand what they are trying to say, but not otherwise. If something comes to mind, make a note of it, to enable you to remember it when the speaker has finished.

Listening is crucial. The appraisal is not a forum for the boss to put forward their views about how the world should be put to rights. It is the forum for the boss to listen to the employee, take note of what is being said, and respond appropriately.

Empathy

A good interviewer or interviewee will always try to appreciate the other person's point of view, to try understand what they are saying. This leads to empathy between the parties, and an increased likelihood of goodwill and success.

THE PURPOSES OF THE INTERVIEW

As already discussed, these may include:

◆ establishing training needs;

◆ assessing past performance and providing appropriate praise or criticism;

◆ setting targets for future performance;

◆ determining suitability for promotion or transfer;

◆ assessing future potential.

Other purposes may be necessary. Within the general agreed framework, each party may wish to raise specific points. For example the appraisee may wish to complain about poor supervision. It is useful if the appraiser knows this point will be raised in order to prepare an answer for it.

FINDING BACKGROUND INFORMATION

Some questions may need further preparation on the part of the other party. It is better if the information is ready at the time of the appraisal interview. If you know the appraisee has a problem with supervision before the interview takes place, you can look into the possible reasons behind it. In the interview itself you are only going to hear the appraisee's side of the argument, and it would be extremely unwise to base any decisions on partial data. Before the interview takes place, go and see the appraisee's supervisor (assuming it is not you) and get their view.

Important

If you are the supervisor, reflect on why there might be a problem. The important thing here is to allow the discussion to take place. If you are the supervisor do not personalise the situation, you are work colleagues, not friends. You have to work together, not socialise or be part of the same family. It is important to separate out the personal from the professional.

The supervisor may not realise there is a problem, and a chat may solve it. Perhaps the supervisor is unaware of some personal issue that is affecting the appraisee's performance, such as overtiredness because of a new baby. If the supervisor had been thinking the poor performance was due to laziness, this will cause trouble between the supervisor and the employee. The solution may be very straightforward; be more sympathetic with the appraisee, and perhaps temporarily transfer some of their workload.

Communication is key. Communication is the solution to a high proportion of the problems that can occur between people in organisations. Small problems are solved before they become serious through communication.

In many cases the solution is not simple. If there is a serious personality clash between colleagues, then it may be possible to transfer someone; if not, then another solution will have to be found. Make people aware of the cause of the problem and help them deal with it. The important point is that you make an effort to understand both sides of any problem – preferably before the interview.

PREPARING FOR THE INTERVIEW

It should not be necessary to state that both parties need to be prepared for the appraisal interview, but in real life one or both parties go into the interview not knowing what they are going to say, or how they are going to respond to what the other party is going to say. This may lead to an unsatisfactory outcome.

Once the purposes of the interview have been established, the way to obtain a better outcome is for both parties to work out what information they need to collect for the interview. They should plan their own questions, let the other party know the topics they are wanting to cover, and think about answers to the questions they know the other party is going to ask. This is considered in more detail in the next chapter, because it is key to the appraisal interview. Relevant information should be collected, and a copy of the **pre-appraisal report** (see Chapter 8) prepared and seen by both parties before the interview. The appraiser should take responsibility for ensuring this is completed, though much of the information might come from the appraisee.

A good interview must fulfil certain requirements, some of which are specific to the appraiser. These include:

◆ choosing the right location;

◆ creating a relaxed atmosphere;

◆ asking the right questions;

◆ structuring the interview (some questions are prede-
termined and some may arise from the interview
process);

◆ personal skills;

◆ obtaining and recording data accurately for follow-
up.

Devising and formatting questions

Formatting the questions appropriately is important.
Questions should normally be open-ended, that is, help
the person being interviewed answer in greater detail
than in a simple yes/no fashion. For example, 'Why do
you think your sales figures are lower than usual?' is
better than 'Are your sales figures lower than usual
because you have not been well?' The former leads to
a better discussion. You can respond to the appraisee's
answers with further questions, or prompts, to elicit
further information. Closed questions are fine for
simple information, but are not conducive to exploring
the complexity of the work situation.

BASIC COUNSELLING SKILLS

It is important for you to have basic counselling skills,
though you should never try to take the place of a
professional counsellor. If the individual clearly needs
counselling, then they should be directed towards

experts. The reasons you need counselling skills are that they are useful when carrying out interviews, and you never know when you might need them! While it is best to direct someone to professional help, there will always be occasions when people blurt out the personal problem that is troubling them. Difficult situations will need a display of tact and diplomacy on your part.

You need to be gentle, be empathetic and display good listening skills. Counselling is not a matter of telling someone what to do. While providing good advice is acceptable, and useful, it is up to the individual to decide how to resolve a problem.

Counselling skills may be particularly important if the appraisal concerns either redundancy or the possible transfer to another post. If the appraisee knows the potential consequences of poor performance then the interview might be quite stressful, for both parties.

NEGOTIATING SKILLS

It is important that both parties have good negotiating skills. This may at first sight seem odd – negotiation? But it is important that both parties know how to talk to each other, to try to ensure their position is respected and, preferably, accepted. It is often the case that negotiation leads to a compromise which is acceptable to both parties.

Poor negotiation means that both parties will be dissatisfied with the outcome.

The aim of good negotiation is a win-win situation where, even if both parties start from a different standpoint, they can both feel they have benefited.

Getting a sense of equality

One important prerequisite for good negotiation is a sense of equality between the two parties. This is important for the appraisal. We talked in Chapter Two about the open organisation. One of the principles of the open organisation is that there is a sense of equality; people should be treated as equals in organisations. This is not a trivial point. Everyone should be working towards the same goals, the success of the organisation and the happiness of the people working in the organisation.

The reality is that there are hierarchies in organisations. One person tells another what to do and when to do it. Sometimes this is explicit and highly controlled; in other organisations it is more implicit and less controlling. The appraiser may have a higher status than the appraisee (though this is not always the case). It is often difficult to achieve true equality. If the two parties need to negotiate as equals, then the appraisee must not have to fear any later recriminations for acting without regard to the appraiser's usual status.

It is difficult to attain true equality between individuals of different status within the organisation. Unconscious processes come into play. Appraisees may not put forward their views and ideas openly, or as strongly as they might, and they may also accept ideas from appraisers more readily than they should. The opposite may be true for the appraiser, who may put forward ideas more forcefully, and be less likely to listen properly to the ideas of the appraisee. This illustrates the importance of both parties *consciously* behaving as equals. This will minimise the problem; but it is very difficult to do!

Eight rules for successful negotiation

There are certain rules that should be followed in order to negotiate successfully. Some of these may appear a little harsh, particularly when you are trying to run an interview that is open and fair. Many of the rules may not seem conducive to such behaviour, but remember they are based on strategies used by skilled negotiators bargaining tough deals between organisations. They are not necessarily harsh; it depends on how they are applied. The appraisal interview is a very different situation from negotiating at an organisational level, but the same rules apply. At another level, many of these negotiating skills are also counselling or listening skills.

If both parties are aware of the rules, then misunder-standings are less likely to occur.

The rules are as follows.

1. Avoiding irritators
These include words and phrases that have little positive effect on the negotiation, but irritate the other side. This might include suggesting that your own position is 'fair' when it patently is not, or implying that the other party's position is not fair. This category also include offensive and insulting statements, or statements based on incomplete information: for example, if you tell the appraisee they are 'incompe-tent' because they have not achieved certain targets, without looking into the reasons why the targets have not been met.

2. Avoiding counter-proposals
Here, one side makes a suggestion, and the other side makes a counter-suggestion, totally ignoring the sug-gestion from the other side. This shows that people are not listening. As mentioned earlier, listening is import-ant in any appraisal interview. If one party ignores the other by simply presenting its own position, it is not listening. For instance, the appraisee may say, 'I have not achieved my targets because the reports have not reached me on time.' The appraisee is suggesting that

there is a communication problem within the organisation. Instead of agreeing to look into the matter, you may simply suggest that the targets have not been reached because the appraisee does not manage time effectively, and so you recommend a time management course. In other words, you have not listened.

3. Avoiding aggressive behaviour

Do not allow the interview to become heated; try to avoid conflict and hostility. If this happens, the situation can quickly get out of control. Fortunately, unless there are pre-existing problems, or one party upsets the other, this is not likely to happen in an appraisal. It is important to ensure that disagreements do not become open conflict. Aggression will not benefit anyone in the appraisal situation. Aggression closes communication.

4. Avoiding argument dilution

'Argument dilution' occurs when one person justifies a position by using too many supporting arguments. This is a self-defeating process as the more arguments one uses in support of a position, the more likely it is that the other party can effectively argue against that position, by turning any one of the supporting arguments around. Once one argument collapses, the whole position may collapse.

For instance, the appraisee may argue that they need a particular type of training, using a whole string of arguments to support their position, such as increased productivity, benefits outweighing costs, efficiency, increased knowledge base and the future potential of the individual. The organisation – the appraiser – may not be able to argue against most of these reasons, but may not believe the appraisee is likely to stay long enough to justify the increased outlay. So the final argument, future potential, can be used against the appraisee to justify not spending resources on training. Thus the appraisee, instead of providing a list of solid reasons why the training should be provided, has undermined their own postion by presenting too many reasons.

Behaviour labelling

This is a technique used to keep the discussion rational, and to slow it down. It involves tagging statements with **prior indicators** that show what the individual is going to say. For instance, instead of saying, 'I would like a pay rise', the appraisee might say, 'I'm going to say something you might not like. I would like a pay rise.' This technique, though it may seem odd on paper, is useful a) when the discussion seems to be losing direction and the person wants to get the interview focused, and b) when issues are being covered too rapidly, and one party wants to slow things down a little to show the listener that the speaker understands their potential response – eg 'you may not like this'. This is a simple but effective technique.

6. Testing understanding and summarising

This is used to ensure that one party has understood what the other person is trying to say, and to give themselves time to think of a response. If the appraiser has suggested a proposal, and the appraisee wishes to clarify it, it is useful if they repeat it in their own words and check with the appraiser to ensure they have understood properly.

For example, if the discussion has centred on training needs, the appraiser should sum up by stating in simple terms the agreed training needs of the appraisee. For example, 'It seems that you would benefit from a course on report writing, which would improve the quality of your writing and ensure reports reach your supervisor on time. Would you agree with that?' Perhaps the information was incomplete, as the appraisee responds, 'I do agree, but you have not mentioned my need for training in time management that we discussed before.'

7. Seeking information

Suppose the other party has put forward a proposal, but has not fully explained their position. The good negotiator will ask for clarification, for the further information required. This is also a useful strategy for controlling the situation. A carefully directed question will steer the discussion in a particular direction. 'I know you are unhappy in the sales department, and you say you have a talent for marketing. Would you explain to me exactly why you believe you are more suited to the marketing department? What is this talent?'

8. Feelings commentary

This describes the way individuals express their feelings. Effective negotiators are more likely to express the way they feel than ineffective negotiators. In the case of appraisal, if the appraiser express their feelings – and are perhaps openly critical of some aspect of the organisation – they may, in the right circumstances, be more likely to obtain the trust of the appraisee. It shows that you are willing to let your guard down, and this in turn makes the other party more likely to state their position openly. On the positive side, this is an important aspect of counselling; on the negative, it is open to abuse.

JOB ANALYSIS

A key element of being an appraiser is job analysis. This is considered in more detail in Chapter 5. If there is no adequate job description available, a job analysis may need to be carried out before the appraisal. This demonstrates how the appraisal system should not be considered separately from other human resource issues. By analysing the job of the appraisee you will learn about that job in great detail. You will become aware of:

◆ how the job is carried out;

◆ the objectives that are reasonable to set someone performing the job;

◆ the limitations on performance imposed by the job;

◆ how the job might need to be changed;

◆ the context of the job within the organisation.

There are numerous techniques of job analysis, some more complex than others. Job analysis is very time-consuming. You will not usually have to go through the whole process. In more efficient organisations, up-to-date and complete job descriptions will be on hand, but the good appraiser should not always rely on this information being available. There is no point in using a job description that is out of date (and they can become out of date very quickly, as we have seen). The information may be wrong. The best way to find out whether a job description is out of date is to ask the person doing the job. In a later chapter we will explore the role of the appraisal in updating job descriptions.

OTHER IMPORTANT SKILLS

Effective use of data

You must use available data effectively, be able to consider various options and to put these options to the appraisee in a reasonable manner. This involves skill and tact. You could simply set high targets and tell the appraisee to achieve them. It is more difficult, but more effective, to sell the objectives to the appraisee, to show them how the objectives are reasonable. It is better still to get the appraisee to provide the objectives themselves, because then they are far more likely to be met. The appraisee will internalise the objectives, accept them implicitly and be more willing to act on them.

Constructive criticism

If an appraisee needs to be criticised then it should be in a positive manner. It is easy to criticise someone's work, but it is harder to criticise without isolating the appraisee and losing their trust, and hence motivation. Do not spend the whole interview tearing apart the appraisee's work. That is hardly conducive to motivating someone! Apart from disillusioning the victim it is also a waste of time. If there is a need to criticise then do so in a reasonable and constructive manner, following up with constructive suggestions as to how to improve things. For instance, if a manager is always rushing around trying to organise things without seeming to get anything done, it is right that they should be criticised. But if this is followed up by the constructive proposal that they should attend a time management course, then the criticism becomes productive.

A firm manner

You do need a certain firmness of manner, which should be used at appropriate times. It is for you to keep the interview on course, to keep to the planned structure of the interview where appropriate, not allowing serious irrelevant diversions. If the interview is going astray, you should bring it back to the topic in question. Firmness of manner means assertiveness, not aggression. It means ensuring you keep control of the situation – not the person – always politely, but always with authority.

Discretion

It is essential that you are discreet. The appraisee must be able to trust you to keep whatever is discussed confidential. They will be more open if they trust you not to reveal anything to others that you have said in confidence.

Objective judgements

You should be able to make objective judgements based on accurate data in an unbiased fashion. This is not always easy, especially if you are the appraisee's supervisor and there is antagonism between you; but you must rise above such feelings, which have no role in the open organisation.

Questionnaires, rating scales

You may need to design and analyse supervisor and other kinds of ratings. On many occasions, these will be designed and analysed by someone else. This is a specialist skill; and not one to be undertaken lightly. This involves:

- designing supervisor/peer/subordinate rating questionnaires that are appropriate to particular circumstances;

- training people to complete them correctly;

- interpreting and analysising them appropriately.

Rating questionnaires are often used as performance indicators. Use them with great caution as ratings are necessarily subjective judgements, and so may be biased (see Chapter 8).

CASE STUDY

Emily Robins was regional sales manager in the Midlands for a large firm of paper manufacturers. She was very happy, she was good at her job and everyone knew it. Her region consistently outperformed other regions, and this was in large part due to her personal efforts. Then Emily was told unofficially by her friend at head office, Clare, that the vacancy for the post of national sales director was going to become vacant soon, and that she was the best candidate – if she was interested. She was very interested, and when the post was advertised she applied immediately.

Things then started to go wrong. When she heard nothing for a few weeks, she telephoned Clare to find out what was happening. Clare was evasive, and said that the directors had not considered the applications yet. So Emily waited for another couple of weeks. Finally, she received a letter which said that unfortunately she had not got the post, but thank you for applying.

Emily was livid. She repeatedly phone head office for an explanation but got nowhere. She felt rejected by the organisation and this showed in her work, which deteriorated considerably. After a couple of months, during which time she was far from happy, she was called to head office for her appraisal. The appraiser was one of the directors, Neil Kent.

The interview was heated. Neil knew that Emily had been turned down for the head office post in favour of someone from outside the organisation who was very experienced at this level. What he was not prepared for was the level of Emily's anger. When he told Emily why she had not got the job she just managed to control her temper and explained that she felt the company had let her down very badly, that after so many years experience they had not even interviewed her for the job – though she was supposedly the best candidate, and she was certainly well-qualified – and they had then refused to discuss with her the reasons why she had not got the post. As the company was only interested in talking to her now they saw weaknesses in her performance it was obvious they still did not care about her needs. Two weeks later, after careful consideration and with the offer of a better job elsewhere, Emily resigned.

Comment

Emily was obviously very valuable to the company, and they ended up losing her. She had attained the status of regional sales manager and was performing very well. They did not want to lose her. When the national vacancy arose it is unfortunate that they did not even interview her. There are potentially legal implications here. If she fulfilled the requirements of the job specification then she should have been interviewed. If she did not then, because of her status in the organisation if for no other reason, she should have been told why. She should have been given the reasons why she did not get the job and then been provided, through the appraisal procedure, the means to develop so she would be ready for promotion. It is important that organisations show that they value the individual. In this case they did not, so they lost a good, productive worker.

$$\left(\begin{array}{c}5\end{array}\right)$$

Describing the job, describing the person

In this chapter:

◆ **Job analysis**

◆ **Job description**

◆ **Person specification**

This chapter examines the role of the job analysis, job description and person specification, and how they are used in the appraisal, such as ensuring that the person is doing all aspects of the job, or examining how the job is changing over time because of the appraisee's specific skills or interests. Including job analysis in the appraisal will enable the employer and the employee to see how the job is changing over time. This is particularly important in more fluid and developing organisations. It will help identify training needs, and also to determine whether new job roles are necessary.

The procedures described in this chapter relate to areas much wider than appraisal, and there are many stable jobs where such issues are irrelevant, as they do not fundamentally change for many years. This chapter is important where there are significant organisational or job changes occurring, as appraisal can be one key area where consultation between the employee and the employer can take place. If jobs are to change, then the employee should have a significant say in how they are to change.

INTRODUCTION TO JOB DESCRIPTIONS

The job description should not be a fixed, never-changing document. It will need to evolve in response to the needs of the organisation and the aims of the individual employee. There is enormous scope for abuse of the system here. If the organisation is not trusted then employees will worry that their job descriptions, and hence their contracts, will be altered without consultation. Contracts should not be altered without consultation with and, where possible, the agreement of, the employee (there are legal limits to such changes, as well as moral ones). On the other hand, the individual employee may want their job description to change; they may want to take on new responsibilities and new challenges. If this fits within the aims of the organisation then this should be encouraged. Finally, the nature of a job may naturally change over time. A job description that once applied may evolve to be a very different job several years later, and it may have happened with no one noticing – even the employee!

For these reasons, the job description is occasionally part of the appraisal process. That does not mean it must be actively updated every time there is an appraisal, but it should be considered regularly for the benefit of both the employee and the organisation. If the organisation does not know that the job description has implicitly changed, then it will not be aware of the job that is being done – which cannot aid efficiency. On the other hand, if the employee is carrying out activities not explicitly recognised on the job description then they may be carrying responsibilities for which they are not being rewarded.

Developing job descriptions

The process of developing a job description from scratch is usually rather laborious, and will be outlined here only because it aids the process relevant to the appraisal system, that of adapting and updating the job description. There are three areas:

◆ job analysis;

◆ job description;

◆ and person specification.

Fitting the person specification to the job description is important because it will show where there might be problems. Over time a mismatch may develop between the person and the job, demonstrating that the person may have training and development needs in order to rectify the anomaly.

If, after the appraisal has taken place, a new job description has been agreed, then full details should be sent to the human resources department (or the person responsible for personnel) to ensure that the new tasks or responsibilities fit within the band or grade of the post. If not, then a new band or grade may have to be negotiated. Changing the job description is a major procedure, and should not be undertaken lightly. Legal issues must be accounted for.

The development of the job description involves going about systemically collecting, analysing and documenting the important elements of a job. The job description is not just about what the person does, but how this fits in with the strategic aims of the organisation.

JOB ANALYSIS

The first stage of developing a full job description is that of the job analysis. There are various means of carrying out a job analysis, of varying degrees of complexity. These are beyond the scope of this book. One of the simpler and more effective types of job analysis is called task analysis, which is carried out to determine exactly what tasks need to be done in order for the job to be carried out effectively. The task analysis involves analysing the job to identify:

◆ what tasks are carried out;

◆ how long they take;

◆ how often they are carried out.

◆ which tasks are critical to the job, and which are carried out by the employee for other reasons.

There are various ways of obtaining this information (many of which are used in other forms of job analysis):

◆ Check whether a job description already exists. If there is not a detailed one there may be a summary one that has been used for advertising purposes. Remember that just because a job description exists does not mean that it is up-to-date.

- Observe the job being done. This is time-consuming, and may not be practical for many jobs, but it does provide a detailed account of the job.

- Ask the appraisee to keep a diary of tasks carried out over a period of a few weeks. These can then be analysed in terms of frequency, time taken, etc.

- Interview the people doing the job. If you have gathered any of the information above, use this in order to improve the task analysis (interviewing more than one person may indicate which elements of the job are being carried out by which people; not everyone will necessarily do every task).

- Interview the supervisor.

If you wish to carry out more sophisticated forms of job analysis there are various published questionnaire methods available, often computer-based. Contact the British Psychological Society (see Useful Addresses at end of book for contact details) for further information. Tests focus on a range of tasks, output, context and personal attributes in order to develop person specifications. If you are going to use such sophisticated tools, it may be wise (indeed, it may be necessary) to employ a psychologist to ensure the questionnaires are used properly.

Assessing tasks

While some jobs involve just a few repetitive tasks, most jobs involve a range of activities. And this is not just restricted to white collar management and professional jobs. For instance, lorry drivers do not just drive lorries. They will have to know how to load and unload, tie ropes and sheets, know the basics of being a mechanic, read a map, perhaps speak foreign languages (for continental drivers), interact effectively with customers, suppliers, warehouse personnel and others – this may involve negotiation, counselling and management skills. And the list goes on. An employer doesn't just employ someone with a lorry driving licence; they need to know that they can carry out this range of tasks as well.

The process of task analysis will involve finding out details of the tasks from the people doing the job, their supervisors, and the people they interact with – not forgetting to look at previous job descriptions of similar jobs. The job analysis does not just list the tasks, it should consider the kinds of skills and aptitudes required of a person carrying out the task, along with any personality characteristics that might be important. This will help later when devising the person specification. An example of a job analysis form is shown in Figure 1.

Tasks	Knowledge/skills	Personality/aptitudes
1		
2		
3		
4		
5		
N		

Figure 1. Example of a task analysis form.

In order to identify the key elements of the job, ask the supervisor to record **critical incidents.** Ask them to recall incidents that showed someone doing the job in an excellent manner, and others that showed them doing it badly. These incidents will show which elements of the job are crucial and also help devise the person specification, described later in the chapter.

Task analysis: explanatory notes

This checklist (Figure 1) is used in conjunction with the job description and person specification. It enables the appraiser to analyse the skills, aptitude and personality characteristics required. It is often useful to obtain help filling it in from people doing the job and their supervisors.

The task analysis is used for designing the job description and person specification. The questionnaire is split into three columns: task, knowledge/skills and personality/aptitudes.

Task

The individual tasks carried out by the appraisee are entered here. If possible, include a percentage figure for each task indicating the time spent on it. If this is not done, then it may mistakenly be assumed that all tasks are equally important, and this may be misleading.

Knowledge/skills

What knowledge and skills are required for each task? This is a very important column, and may include educational qualifications, knowledge of a geographical area, skills obtained at work.

Personality/aptitudes

These are the characteristics a person may have in order to do the job effectively. Some tasks require a certain level of general ability, or specific aptitudes, eg mechanical or numerical ability. Some tasks may be carried out more effectively if the person has particular personality characteristics or ways of dealing with people. For instance, if people are working in a team, it will be beneficial to have some teamworking ability.

JOB DESCRIPTION

The job description is developed from the job analysis.

It is the job description that is sent out to potential applicants for a job so it must accurately portray the tasks and responsibilities of the job. It is also the job description that may be adapted during the appraisal process.

Once we have completed the job analysis it can be relatively straightforward to complete the job description. This involves not only a description of the tasks that a person does, but how the job relates to other jobs in the organisation, and how it fits with the overall strategic aims of the organisation. It will usually include:

◆ the specific job functions or tasks, including those which are essential and those which are desirable;

◆ the percentage of time spent on each task (in many cases this is variable, but it provides a useful indication to job applicants);

◆ a summary of the skills, aptitudes and personality characteristics required;

◆ the physical and mental requirements;

◆ any special conditions of employment;

◆ supervision received and exercised.

A job description handed to an applicant will also include details of salary, hours worked, etc. For the purposes of the appraisal the above is likely to be adequate when considering ways in which the job description may need to be adapted and changed over time.

The job description is used in the appraisal to help determine performance and also to consider the role of the job within the organisation, to provide an organisational check on the job that is actually done compared with the job description that is provided. While in one way the latter is not part of the appraisal, it is in the sense that if there is a discrepancy between the job description and the job the person is doing then one of the purposes of the appraisal is to find out why. It may be that the appraisee is inadvertently omitting a particular task, or it may be that the task is either being done elsewhere or has ceased to be necessary. The appraisee is in a good position to say what is happening. See Figure 2 for an example of a job description form.

Job description: explanatory notes
It is crucial to understand the nature and purpose of the job. The job description is used in order to define the job characteristics, the tasks involved, and the personal characteristics required of the person doing

Job Description

Job title: Department:

Date: Prepared by:

Responsible to:

Responsible for:

Positions from which people might be promoted/transferred to this job:

Avenues of promotion/transfer from this post:

Main tasks:

Subsidiary tasks:

Summary of skills/aptitudes/personality characteristics required:

Physical requirements of job:

Conditions of employment:

Figure 2. Example of a job description form.

the job. The following notes will help you complete the job description form.

Basic details
The initial information provides basic information about the post.

Responsibility and position of post
This shows who the person is responsible for, who they are responsible to, and possible routes of transfer and

promotion. This helps place the job within the context of the organisation, and provides useful information for training and development in the appraisal.

Main and subsidiary tasks

These show the tasks the person is expected to carry out, along with some indication of the proportion of time the person is expected to spend on them.

Personal characteristics

This may include qualifications and training, aptitudes and ability, and personal characteristics that may be conducive to good job performance.

Physical requirements

This may be necessary for some jobs, and may include physical strength, good eyesight, good colour vision.

Conditions of employment

This can include hours worked, salary, the environment in which the job is worked.

THE PERSON SPECIFICATION

The person specification describes the individual abilities and characteristics needed for the job, based on the job description and the task analysis. There is no single ideal person for any job. The reason why psychological research into the relationship between personality and particular jobs has been unsuccessful is that people with broadly different characteristics will perform just as well in the job. The person specification picks out key skills, abilities and characteristics which contribute towards effective job performance. They include skills, abilities and characteristics which are:

◆ essential for good performance;

◆ desirable for good performance;

◆ conflicting with good performance, ie if the person has this characteristic then it is likely that they will perform poorly in the job because of it.

Six main headings

The person specification includes different sorts of information about the individual, categorised into six headings. The information obtained under each heading must be relevant to the job. Irrelevant information is not included, as it may bias the specification. Bear in mind that people with very different characteristics can be successful in jobs. In many cases there will be little or no information under some headings. The six headings are as follows.

1. Qualifications

Educational background, including vocational training and qualifications, skills.

2. Intelligence/aptitudes

The level of general ability or specific ability, such as numerical or verbal, manual dexterity, etc.

3. Personality

As mentioned above, different kinds of personality types are often successful at a given job, but there may be general characteristics which may be desirable (or conflicting), such as emotional stability, dominance, sociability, aggressiveness.

4. Interests

Sometimes free time activities or hobbies are relevant to the job. How does the person want to develop in the future? Are their interests primarily artistic, social, practical, entrepreneurial? This is an area where you must ensure you do not include irrelevant information.

5. Motivation

Is the ideal candidate for the job likely to be motivated by money, social standing, status, praise?

6. Appearance/circumstances

This might include information on build, tidiness of dress, speech. It can include family factors. It is the area you must be most careful about because of the law. You cannot usually discriminate on the basis of sex, race, disability or age. Do not include information unless it is strictly necessary.

It is helpful when devising the person specification to use a checklist like the one shown in Figure 3. You can then, using the job description already designed, and perhaps with further help from people doing the job and their supervisors, fill in the checklist.

Job title:	Department:		
Date:	Prepared by:		
	Essential	**Desirable**	**Conflicting**
1. Qualifications			
2. Intelligence/aptitudes			
3. Personality			
4. Interests			
5. Motivation			
6. Appearance/circumstances			

Figure 3. Person specification.

The information for the person specification is placed under one of the three headings:

- **Essential**: the qualities placed under this heading are considered essential for the proper performance of the job. It is important not to have more essential qualities than necessary or it may be impossible to find anyone who meets the specification

- **Desirable**: qualities that would be useful in the applicant, but not essential.

- **Conflicting**: a very useful category. It is often important to indicate characteristics that would make people positively unsuitable.

When using the checklist, the appraiser should try to include at least one characteristic for each of the six headings (ie a minimum of six, rather than 18, characteristics), as this will help describe the 'ideal person' more accurately.

Examples of the use of the person specification

Examples of the six headings include:

- **Qualifications**: a teacher needs an appropriate degree; a bricklayer should be time-served; sales staff might need general education to GCSE or A level standard, but no particular subjects.

- **Intelligence/aptitude**: a component assembler in a factory needs manual dexterity; a bank manager needs a facility for numbers; a lorry driver needs spatial intelligence.

◆ **Personality**: a salesperson may need to be an extrovert, and perhaps resilient (so they are not affected by rebuttals); a self-employed person needs self-discipline, a diver needs courage.

◆ **Interests**: a scientist must be interested in novelty; an engineer needs an interest in mechanical devices; a teacher should be interested in having a broad general knowledge.

◆ **Motivation**: a salesperson is likely to be motivated by money, by the amount of commission on a sale; a gardener is likely to be motivated by the results of the work; a university lecturer may be motivated by an intrinsic interest in the subject matter.

◆ **Appearance/circumstances**: a shop manager may have to dress in a suit, as would an accountant or solicitor; lorry drivers' families may have to accept that they will stay away overnight several times a week.

Note the change in language across some of these. With qualifications there is a certainty, a lorry driver has to have a lorry driving licence, a teacher has to have a degree; but when it comes to motivation or personality, there is less certainty. These are just indications that the person *may* have certain qualities.

APPRAISAL, JOB DESCRIPTION AND PERSON SPECIFICATION

The appraisal makes use of the job description and person specification for two purposes:

1. For the organisation, to ensure the details are up-to-date, that if people need to be employed in the job the job description and person specification are appropriate.

2. For the individual appraisee, to ensure that they are effectively carrying out all aspects of the job, that the organisation is recognising the tasks they do (if they are working beyond the job description they may require further reward), and that they will be provided with appropriate training to ensure they are carrying out the job effectively.

Having the job description and person specification to hand when carrying out an appraisal can be very useful, as they will indicate particular areas of discussion and debate. The appraiser can concentrate on areas where there appears to be a mismatch. A mismatch does not mean that the person is unsuited to the post. It could be that the mismatch is in the other direction, that they are doing more than is necessary, so they may need further reward. If there is a problem, it could be rectified by training.

Important

You must always allow for the person specification being incomplete and less than comprehensive. People are individuals, and should be treated as such. They have widely varying skills, abilities and characteristics. If there is a mismatch between the person and the specification, do not assume it is the person at fault. It is easy to be too specific and controlling by misapplying the job description and person specification.

A key management tool

The person specification can be a key part of the appraisal interview, where performance is assessed and targets set. This is because:

◆ it may help determine why the appraisee has failed to reach particular targets;

◆ it will help both parties get to the root of the problem more quickly;

◆ it is useful when assessing the appraisee's training requirements with regard to the job.

CASE STUDY

Devising the job description

Charles Turner has been given responsibility for all marketing personnel. Part of his work involves appraising everyone in the department. Wanting to be thorough, he wishes to update the relevant job descriptions before carrying out any appraisals. Unfortunately his managers do not see things the same way. If he is going to update all the relevant job descriptions properly then he is going to spend a large amount of time at his desk, and enlist the help of others. The company does not like the idea of Charles spending some weeks on this task.

This leaves Charles responsible for something he cannot now carry out to the best of his ability. Charles must use the information he has, which consists of short generic job descriptions used for advertising purposes.

To get round the problem, Charles devises a questionnaire that can be filled in by all marketing personnel. The questionnaire brings together information on task analysis, job description, and person specification; and he intends to use the answers as a basis for the appraisal discussions. Because people do not like completing forms, Charles partially completes them using information he has to hand. Then, when an appraisal is due, he asks the appraisee to complete the questionnaire, indicating whether the presented information is correct, and what should be amended.

Comment

Organisations are not always willing to employ the appropriate resources for a task. Using this method Charles circumvents the organisation, obtains a fairly clear idea of the different jobs carried out in the marketing department, and has information useful for appraisal preparation; all without unduly upsetting the employees with a long-winded, time-consuming questionnaire. He is now in a position to carry out more effective appraisals.

6

Alternative appraisals

In this chapter:

+ **The various types of appraisal**

+ **Working with teams**

+ **Timing**

+ **Regular versus continuous appraisal**

TYPES OF APPRAISAL

Most appraisals consist of an annual meeting between the line manager and the appraisee. This chapter briefly examines the alternatives to this traditional approach.

PAY-RELATED APPRAISAL

Many organisations link appraisal to pay, usually through a performance-related pay (PRP) system. This is where the employee receives pay increases or bonuses wholly or partly on the basis of the regular and systematic assessment of job performance through a system of performance review.

While most of this book attempts to separate pay and appraisal, and focuses on ensuring the perspective of the individual employee is heard, the reality is that appraisal, in many organisations, is related to pay. There is a tendency towards a closer link between pay and appraisal, ie appraisal is only about assessing performance, both in the public and private sectors. There are circumstances where such a system is beneficial and appropriate; but there is a worrying trend towards pay-related appraisal being introduced in situations where it is very difficult, if not impossible, to create objective performance measures (eg management and professional work). In these cases I would encourage organisations not to link performance too closely to pay, as there are many potential pitfalls, and it is very difficult – if not impossible – to create a fair system.

If objective measures are not available, then reward will be in the hands of the appraiser. Subjective and possibly arbitrary reward systems are not conducive to good relationships between workers and management. The situation will be exacerbated where there is a poor relationship between the appraisee and the appraiser. There will then be appeals against decisions, with all the waste and unhappiness they engender.

In many organisations performance is not an individual matter. Most of us depend on the performance of others in order to perform our own jobs well, whether that is other members of a team or department, or the way the work is managed. Performance can often only be seen as a collective process, and any rewards can only be given in a collective manner. One PRP scheme I saw was in a university where all the money for the PRP for a particular faculty was distributed evenly amongst all staff. This ensured everyone had an annual bonus, and people were more likely to feel satisfied working within the faculty. It was fairer than some systems.

What characteristics do appraisal-related pay schemes need?

- They emphasise the importance of effective individual job performance (bear in mind that performance is not always linked to any particular individual).

- They relate to targeting resources.

- They will either help retain and motivate employees – or just the opposite.

- Systems must be individually-designed for particular organisations.

- They require objective and appropriate criteria – this means that many organisations should not consider introducing such systems.

Pros and cons of PRP

In certain circumstances, PRP can benefit both employers (through improved performance) and employees (through increased pay). In some types of organisation, appraisal-related pay will have flexibility, and will motivate employees to work harder, and hence target higher pay at better performers.

PRP works best where performance can be objectively measured, either for an individual or for a team. There are certain industries where PRP provides a genuine incentive to people to worker harder, and where job satisfaction is increased through such financial rewards. If PRP increases both satisfaction and productivity then it is acceptable.

A poorly-designed appraisal system will demotivate employees. Employees need to understand the system. They also need to know that the advantages are applied consistently and fairly across all people. There may be a problem if the organisation emphasises the importance of teamwork rather than the autonomy of individuals. How should the team be rewarded? Should all members of a team receive equal rewards? Are the members of the team rewarded fairly? How can a system with teams be fair? Trade unions are often hostile towards PRP schemes because they are seen as running counter to the principles of collective bargaining. The way to overcome these objections is to apply the system appropriately, use objective and fair performance criteria, and ensure equal opportunity of access to rewards.

Introducing a system

Introducing an appraisal-related pay scheme can be expensive. Larger organisations are more likely to introduce one. Because of the costs, many organisations only consider introducing such schemes for senior management before cascading the system down to other employees. An organisation needs to consider whether introducing such a system might have a negative outcome in the sense of creating resentment among employees who do not have access to these benefits. Introducing such a system with managers also has the danger that it is very difficult to create objective criteria for managers.

SELF-APPRAISAL

There are advantages to having employees appraise themselves:

◆ It can help enhance their self-respect within the organisation because they are being given responsibility for their own work.

- It is likely to increase commitment to organisational and personal goals.

- It can be an effective motivator.

The system works by appraisees taking responsibility to rate themselves on all the main tasks in their job, commenting on strengths and weaknesses, and identify their own training and development needs. This is then used as the basis for a discussion with the appraiser. This is different from normal appraisal in that the appraisee takes full responsibility for the content of the pre-appraisal report and the content and format of the appraisal. The appraisee controls the interview, asks the questions, and helps management to ensure that their job is effective and satisfactory.

Unfortunately there is a serious downside to the use of self-ratings. Studies comparing supervisor ratings with self-ratings show – unsurprisingly – people rate themselves higher than do supervisors. This is particularly true for managerial and professional groups compared to manual workers. It is also necessary to ensure that the appraisal discussion is two-way. The appraisee may not have identified particular issues that are important to the organisation. The appraiser must be able to raise these issues.

PEER APPRAISAL

Peer appraisal, the assessment of the individual by people working in the same job, will be considered in more detail in the next chapter, as part of the 360 degree appraisal. It is useful for people who work in a team, and it will provide useful information about how people work together. There is always the danger of bias, particularly if the organisation is dysfunctional. An open organisation is ideal for peer appraisal, but one which is distrustful should not use peer appraisal. There is evidence that individuals rate others similar to themselves higher than those who are dissimilar. They are also likely to rate friends higher than non-friends. There may be systematic bias against particular individuals because they 'do not fit'.

On the other hand, research has shown that peer assessments are more stable than supervisor assessments, and that they are more likely to focus on the appraisee's performance than on effort. They are also good at making accurate predictions regarding future performance.

Belbin's team roles

A useful method of examining how teams work together that has been used for many years is that of Belbin's team roles, which can be used in team appraisals. Belbin based his research on the interaction of several hundred teams which conducted management team games, and proposed a theory that there are nine different types of role. We all have a mix of roles, some stronger than others, and an awareness of our role preference is helpful when carrying out team appraisals.

The roles are:

- **Co-ordinator**: a person-oriented leader. This person is trusting, accepting, dominant, and is committed to team goals and objectives. A positive thinker, the co-ordinator approves of effort in others. They are tolerant, willing to listen to others, but also strong enough to reject their advice. The co-ordinator does not stand out as a dominant leader, and does not necessarily lead through a sharp intellect.

- **Shaper**: a person with a lot of energy, who focuses on the task. A shaper has a high motivation to achieve. They help shape others into achieving the aims of the team. They may be aggressive. More than one shaper in a team can create problems.

- **Plant**: the ideas person who has a high IQ. They may be introverted yet also dominant and original. A plant will take a radical approach to the way the team works and to solving problems. They are not usually concerned with the details of the problem.

They are argumentative and may lose interest once the idea has been explored. They do not follow through.

- **Resource investigator**: this is the person who is constantly exploring possibilities and opportunities, developing contacts, and exploring resources outside the team. They are good negotiators who talk to others to gain information; they pick up other people's ideas (eg the plant) and develop them. They are sociable and enthusiastic. On the other hand, they tend to have few original ideas, and may lose interest after the initial exploration of the idea.

- **Company worker/implementer**: these people are aware of obligations, both to the team and outside, and are disciplined and conscientious. They are tough-minded, practical, trusting, tolerant, and they have a respect for established traditions. They tend to be calm and work for the team in a practical way. Implementers are often in positions of responsibility in organisations. They can be good at doing the jobs others do not want to do, such as discipline. They are conservative, inflexible and not good at responding to new possibilities.

- **Monitor-evaluator**: these tend to be prudent, intelligent people with a low need for achievement. They are good at evaluating competing proposals, so are useful at the point of decision-making though they are slow at coming to a decision, because it is important to them not to be wrong. Monitor-evaluators are not affected by emotional arguments; they are serious-minded. At times they may appear boring or over-critical. They are not good at inspiring others.

- **Team worker**: these tend to be good at averting potential friction in the team, and help the more difficult members use their skills towards more positive ends. They tend to keep team spirit up and help others to contribute effectively. They have diplomatic skills and tend to use humour. They are able to listen, they cope with awkward people, and are sociable, sensitive and person-oriented. They also tend to be indecisive and reluctant to say things which might hurt other people.

- **Completer-finishers**: these people dot the 'i's and cross the 't's. They pay attention to detail, and they are very thorough. They work steadily and are consistent. They have little interest in being recognised for success. They may be over-anxious and are unable to delegate effectively.

- **Specialist**: this person provides the specialist knowledge and skills required to solve tasks. They tend to be introverted and anxious, but self-starting and dedicated to the task. They show little interest in other people and are single-minded.

Belbin devised a questionnaire which is easily and quickly completed which enables people to identify which roles they prefer. Using this information, team managers can play to the strengths of individual members of the team and recognise areas where individuals are weaker.

UPWARD APPRAISALS

Very few organisations use upward appraisal. There are two main reasons for this. First, the approach is incompatible with the managerial styles of many organisations, where there are clear distinctions between manager and worker. Second, there is a fear that such appraisals may undermine managerial power.

An open organisation welcomes upward appraisal. Workers should get the opportunity to comment on the management styles of their managers; to examine their strengths and weaknesses. It provides a good opportunity to show where a manager might need assistance or training. Workers and team members can comment on a range of matters, such as the effectiveness of managers regarding:

- delegation;

- communication (both written and oral);

- leadership;

- ability to feed back on performance;

- guidance and advice;

- recognition of individual needs;

- consultation;

- interpersonal relationships.

Workers are in a good position to observe management behaviour. It is important that workers get the opportunity to comment, such a system is compatible with the open organisation. There are specific keys that will help make upward ratings work:

- participative management style;

- rater anonymity;

- behaviour-specific items.

Upward appraisal is useful because it helps improve management skills. Such skills are usually only imparted through training which involves other managers, professional trainers, and external consultants – all people who do not have to be managed by the manager! There is a danger of circularity if no one below the level of the manager actually assesses their work. It makes sense to consult those people who are most affected by the behaviour of the manager. Upward ratings also focus attention on staff needs; such ratings will identify local organisational problems, such as how staff feel they are treated. Such ratings will also identify managers' strengths, which will assist the manager's appraisal.

The value of the upward appraisal, apart from being able to examine aspects of the manager's job, is that it gives employees a voice, critical to the open organisation, it empowers workers and will enhance their satisfaction and the organisation's effectiveness.

It is usually the case that workers will only be in a position to comment on some aspects of the manager's job, the parts they observe. Again, this is a method that is only effective when used in conjunction with other appraisal methods.

TIMING APPRAISALS: REGULAR VS CONTINUOUS

Appraisals are traditionally carried out once a year, as a check on performance and need. In today's organisations, this is often not enough. The appraisal process has to take account of continual change. The appraisee may be faced with novel situations which are best dealt with through the appraisal system. This does not have to mean the appraisal is overburdening. An 'appraisal interview' can last just a couple of minutes if it occurs in the period between appraisals. Of course, how appraisal works will depend on the organisation. There is no single answer regarding how the appraisal system should run.

Continuous appraisal

For those organisations in which there is regular and perhaps unpredictable change, the annual appraisal is too slow. Appraisal needs to be a continuous process, tied explicitly to training and development programmes. There may be occasions where appraisal meetings need to be held at certain times of the year, or at certain points in the business cycle. A flexible appraisal system, where one party can arrange to meet the other party to discuss important issues at any point in the year, can benefit the organisation.

Weekly or monthly appraisal

This is a less flexible form of the continuous appraisal, but appropriate for many jobs where objective checking is possible. The system can include a card, which contains specific indicators, relating not just to performance, but also to training and development and any other issues that arise. The cards are completed by either the employee or the line manager, and are monitored to ensure that both performance and satisfaction are satisfactory. Cards can include many indicators, perhaps up to 20. If the employee completes the card, these are then moderated by the line manager in discussion with the employee. A close relationship between the manager's appraisal of the employee and their own appraisal should be established as the monitoring occurs monthly.

CONCLUDING COMMENTS

While a range of appraisal systems are acceptable, whichever system you use you should be consistent and reliable. If you have an annual system then you should run the system annually, not leave it for 18 months between appraisals. Such inconsistency will not endear you to your employees. There are many types of appraisal available; what is right for one organisation and one type of employee may not be right for another, so care must be taken over the choice of appraisal which is used.

7

The 360 degree appraisal

In this chapter:

- **When should we use the 360 degree appraisal?**

- **Benefits**

- **Practicalities**

- **Determining the participants**

- **Problems and solutions**

- **Job description/person specification**

WHAT IS A 360 DEGREE APPRAISAL?

The 360 degree appraisal is a good way of addressing training and development needs, both for the appraisee and the organisation. It should only be used in the open organisation. The process entails:

- Convincing management and staff of the efficacy of

the model. Explaining the purpose through discussions and training.

◆ Defining how it will be used, the steps involved in the process.

◆ Designing, distributing, collecting and analysing questionnaires.

◆ Using this information in the appraisal interview.

◆ Providing suitable feedback relating to training and development.

◆ Validating the system.

The new world has rendered traditional boss-down based appraisal extinct.

While this viewpoint might be a little extreme, 360 degree appraisal is becoming more popular, though there are many potential pitfalls. Do not introduce this lightly; do not introduce it into a dysfunctional organisation.

This kind of appraisal has a number of names: reverse appraisal, multi-source feedback, multi-rater feedback or assessment, and full circle appraisal; along with 360 degree appraisal. The last term is the most commonly used, and is the one used here.

As we have seen, traditionally the appraisee's immediate superior, the line manager or supervisor carries out appraisals, so feedback is only obtained from one person – usually the boss. This takes little account of what other people might think. And the boss might be biased! In a culture of equality and openness, appraisal should take a wider context, it should not just be a top-down system, but the appraisee should be assessed by their peers and others (including customers if appropriate) in order to obtain a broader picture of their performance and of training and development needs.

One survey stated that around 8 per cent of companies make use of the 360 degree review, with a further 69 per cent who have plans to implement it in one form or another. These figures will vary enormously according to the size and type of organisation, but the point is that the system is becoming popular.

The 360 degree appraisal is particularly appropriate for open organisations, as it enables an examination not just of the individual but also of the person's interactions with others in the organisation with whom the person interacts, such as managers or subordinates as well as peers, and those outside the organisation the person has regular contact with such as customers. A number of people comment on the appraisee, and this information is collated as part of the appraisal process. The advantage of this is that it has a wider scope than standard appraisals. On the other hand, it will only be successful if there is a high level of trust within the organisation and between colleagues. This is why an open organisation is essential for the 360 degree appraisal.

The 360 degree appraisal involves formalising a natural observation process. Within an organisation we all observe each other, peers, subordinates, managers, and make our own judgements about them – usually informally. We observe people, we form impressions. If we are going to manage this formally through the 360 degree appraisal, we need to be open, trusting and mutually respecting (the open organisation). Interpersonal relationships are very important at work.

360 degree appraisals have been introduced and then discarded by many organisations. This is not because they do not work, it is because they have been implemented and employed inappropriately. The 360 degree appraisal is not appropriate for all appraisal purposes. It is not useful as a tool to help determine pay and promotions. It is a developmental tool. It

should be used constructively to help determine training and development needs.

WHEN SHOULD ORGANISATIONS USE 360 DEGREE APPRAISAL?

The 360 degree appraisal will not work in a command and control hierarchy.

360 degree appraisal should not be used as the only form of appraisal. It is not going to take over from traditional appraisal. It has a wide range of uses but there are limitations. It would not be appropriate to use it for performance review which is linked to pay and promotion. There are too many risks for bias, and co-workers' comments should be used constructively, not working against the appraisee.

One of the reasons 360 degree appraisals have been tried and rejected in many companies is that they have been used too widely. The system falls in and out of favour among organisational psychologists and human resource personnel because it has been used inappropriately, not because it is intrinsically a poor approach to appraisal. There has to be a sense of openness and trust for an organisation to be able to function in a fair way, and this applies particularly to the use of 360 degree appraisals. If the staff work in an environment of mistrust such a system will not work.

360 degree appraisals are a useful mid-year evaluation tool, used as part of a continuous appraisal system. They can be linked to the individual's training and development needs. They are also a useful means of fostering teamwork. Individuals who appraise each other are more likely to assist each other and be aware of each other's strengths, weaknesses and roles within the team.

The 360 degree appraisal should only be used in organisations which have the appropriate size and maturity. Preparing for it is a very big job. Before introducing a 360 degree appraisal, you should consider several factors.

Readiness

Is the organisation ready? Important factors include openness, size, attitude of staff and managers, promoting understanding and support; ensuring the system will be fair, confidential and open. If an organisation is resistant then it can help to start using it either at senior levels (to convince top managers) or as a pilot, to demonstrate to both senior and junior staff that it has benefits.

The 360 degree appraisal will inevitably be intrusive; it is not to be undertaken lightly. It will require a lengthy programme of development. You have to ensure that staff are ready for it.

The 360 degree appraisal will only work in an open organisation, where there is genuine respect between colleagues, high job satisfaction, and an environment where people care about what happens to the organisation.

Consultation

Ask staff what they think about introducing a 360 degree system. Administer a survey for staff to complete, which covers the aims and objectives of the intended appraisal system and how it relates to organisational needs and objectives. This will help generate enthusiasm among staff, once they see that they are involved and that the 360 degree appraisal will benefit them. If there is a pilot study then this may help demonstrate the benefits of the system to staff.

While 360 degree appraisal can be an effective system, it needs to be implemented properly and with care. This kind of appraisal is radical for many people (not least managers), and so any proposal to introduce it might raise concerns among staff. There are a number of factors that can help. These include:

◆ ensuring employees contribute towards the design of the system;

◆ ensuring the system is relatively easy to learn;

- ensuring staff have the opportunity to learn about the system and can have any concerns addressed;

- having a trial of the system properly and providing feedback;

- ensuring confidentiality;

- monitoring the system.

BENEFITS OF THE 360 DEGREE APPRAISAL

This kind of appraisal is particularly useful for:

- instilling trust in the organisation and colleagues;

- a useful extra input about the appraisee, leading to a deeper understanding about how the appraisee is performing and the ways they are perceived by colleagues and customers;

- a counterbalance to results-based performance indicators, reflecting the fact that performance and satisfaction are not just about such indicators, but also about relationships; what they are like and how they can be developed;

- motivating;

- training and development;

- helping people to listen and communicate effectively;

- developing creativity;

- helping to work efficiently as a team;

- teaching when to delegate;

- developing job descriptions and person specifications;

- employee empowerment.

The 360 degree appraisal was originally used only for senior staff. Because of its effectiveness, it has been increasingly used on a wider range of staff – though it is almost exclusively used with management and white collar staff. Modern techniques, such as using computer-based rating scales, have also made it more accessible to a wider range of staff, and cheaper. The surveys used are often more qualitative rather than using a simple rating scale. Qualitative data provide more depth of understanding.

WHEN SHOULD YOU NOT USE 360 DEGREE APPRAISAL?

The 360 degree appraisal is not appropriate in all situations. It is not effective when:

- the person is new to the organisation or to the job;

- there are not enough respondents who understand the scope of the person's responsibilities;

- the organisation is undergoing major change and such an appraisal may lead to confusion;

- as noted above, the organisation is not open, there is mistrust between staff and organisation.

There must be clarity of purpose. 360 degree appraisal is expensive when used properly (and it is only worth using properly), so you should not introduce it without a careful consideration of why you are using it, and who will be part of the system. It might be that you only want to use it for staff development purposes, so you apply it only to people who are being fast-tracked for higher management. The developmental aspect of 360 degree appraisal is very useful, because you obtain direct information from all the groups the appraisee interacts with.

360 degree appraisal will not resolve performance problems, it is a developmental device. It is appropriate to use it as a part of the appraisal system not only for self-development, but also as part of changing the culture of the organisation. If the organisation is a

learning organisation, if it is trying to change positively, then the 360 degree appraisal will indicate the complexity of the changes required or desired.

THE PRACTICALITIES OF THE 360 DEGREE APPRAISAL

Much of the information you need to design the 360 degree appraisal is available elsewhere in this book. The 360 degree appraisal is a matter of collating appropriate information. This will require some thought. You will use a combination of supervisor ratings, peer ratings, upward ratings, ratings from customers or other groups and other forms of information gathered from one or more of these groups (eg team roles from Belbin).

Once the organisation has implemented the appraisal, there are a number of stages relating to who takes part in appraising an individual.

Determining the participants

This will vary, but it will be not only the line manager or supervisor, but co-workers who interact regularly with the appraisee, people in other departments, suppliers and possibly customers. This results in a much broader, more coherent and inclusive picture of the strengths, weaknesses and development needs of the appraisee.

The appraisee chooses three to five people they'd like to get feedback from; the appraiser picks another three to five. This ensures a breadth of coverage. These people should be chosen from the range of people the appraisee interacts with, not necessarily members of the organisation. Fellow employees will normally be suitably qualified to comment on colleagues, though there may be a need for training to ensure that there is consistency.

There are several criteria that should be considered when selecting participants:

- How long have they known the appraisee?

- In what capacity?

- How much contact do they have?

- Do they understand the full nature of what the appraisee does?

- It is important to select some people the appraisee works well with, and some they do not.

Asking the participants for their contribution

The participants are given a short questionnaire and/or asked for comments about the appraisee. The questionnaires should be anonymous. The rating scales should be developed in the same way as described in Chapter Eight. Employees are often nervous about or unwilling to complete questionnaires. Training, and a suitable organisational environment, can help rectify this. There may be problems ensuring the raters complete and return the questionnaires. This can be resolved if the questionnaires are handed out, completed, and returned in one session. That ensures a high response rate.

Some employees may withhold important information, perhaps because they think it might damage the appraisee, perhaps because they think it may damage themselves. If the training has not clarified the purposes of the 360 degree appraisal as a training and development tool – not one to damage the prospects of the participants – then the training is at fault. It has to be emphasised to participants that this system is not about punishment or reward.

There is also a question of ethics, whether it is appropriate to demand that employees complete a form. By the use of appropriate training, employees should accept the system, in which case they are more likely to be willing to complete the form. In the end though, it is difficult to insist that a person completes this kind of form. It should not be treated as a disciplinary procedure.

Presenting the information to the appraisee

These forms are summarised and presented to the appraisee in a constructive manner. Composite scores can be collated from a number of raters. Then, in the same way as a traditional appraisal, this information is used in the appraisal interview. You have to determine the purpose of the data. The analyses should be used for self-reflection, for discussion with the appraiser, the sharing of feedback, and the seeking of clarification where the feedback is ambiguous or unexpected. The appraisee can use it to develop a personal action plan in relation to the ways they deal with other people, and testing this in the future.

The information is used for training and development, for counselling and support. Keep in mind that the 360 degree appraisal is a formalisation of the normal human processes of interpersonal relationships. It also shows how performance is related not just to the individual, but also to the department or the organisation. Performance depends on how people interact with each other, not just how an individual performs alone. This is where the 360 appraisal is effective.

Checking the validity of the system

As is the case for all appraisal systems, the organisation needs to verify the reliability and validity of the system, using the methods described later in the book. It is particularly important to ensure that the rating scales are completed without bias, and that the appraisee recognises the validity of comments made (both positive and negative). It is important to ensure that all major areas are covered by the system.

PROBLEMS AND SOLUTIONS

There are a range of problems that might arise as a result of 360 degree appraisals, and these must be considered and, as far as possible, eliminated before introducing such a system. Such problems might include:

◆ Undermining the authority of the manager. Many professionals will see this as a good thing, but the key issue is that the role of the manager must be clearly understood. 360 degree appraisal will not work in an authoritarian, or perceived authoritarian, organisation.

◆ Employees may be given inappropriate management responsibilities. There may be undue pressure on employees to shoulder responsibility that is not theirs. It is the role of management to provide feedback to enhance a person's effectiveness, not colleagues. This problem is easily resolved because colleagues are not providing the feedback to each other. It remains the manager's job to ensure that the information is collated and summarised, and it is the manager who feeds the information back to the appraisee.

◆ Ratings may be distorted if the system is linked to salary. As stated earlier, 360 degree appraisals should not be linked to salary.

◆ The 360 degree appraisal is effective for looking at the ways appraisees interact with colleagues, how they are seen in relation to the team, whether colleagues believe they are productive, etc, but they cannot provide detailed information on actual productivity. They only provide part of the picture.

◆ There are practical problems relating to ratings scales. It can be difficult to get raters to complete the forms on time. One solution is to have a single session where the forms are handed out, completed, and returned. It is possible that personal biases and prejudices will be displayed through the rating scales. It is important that the raters interpret the scales in a similar manner, only then can useful comparisons be made between appraisees. The appraiser should be in a position to recognise where bias is present. This is not an objective system.

◆ Confidentiality is essential within system. If a rater is not sure that their results will not be available to the appraisee, especially if the appraisee is the boss, then they are less likely to complete the form accurately. It is essential to know who will have access to the data: the external consultant, the appraiser, the boss?

◆ This kind of appraisal can be threatening to staff, it can engender anxiety at all levels within the organisation. Having very negative feedback can be very unpleasant; the appraiser may need to be very skilled to deal with the appraisee's reaction. Negative feedback may indicate that the appraisee should move to another job in a different department. This again indicates that everyone who takes part should be reflexive and sensitive, because their comments can have serious implications for another person's career. For the appraisee, there is a need for an inner strength, an ability to look in the mirror and see ourselves as others see us. People will need an inner strength to deal with negative feedback. This is something that can be learned – to some extent, so good training will be helpful.

◆ There is an inherent contradiction in the 360 degree appraisal. While it has to take place in an open and honest setting, it uses secrecy and anonymity when collecting ratings. Raters subjectively evaluate and judge the work performance of others. Unless the issue is addressed in training this may lead to appraisees resenting being judged by their colleagues. The importance of confidentiality and anonymity must be demonstrated through training. If ratings are not anonymous then people will be less likely to be honest about their evaluations. No matter how open the organisation people are still people, and they behave according to psychological laws. There is a need to protect against false allegations, deceit, retribution for perceived wrongs: the appraisee must be protected against having to answer all individual charges regarding their behaviour. The issues to be addressed should generally be those which are raised by a number of raters; though there will be occasions when a particular issue raised only by a single rater should be addressed. The appraiser or the consultant who prepares the pre-appraisal report should consider which issues are important.

◆ It is important to maintain working relationships. Negative comments and issues arising out of the 360 degree appraisal could potentially prejudice this.

◆ Can people be forced to take part in the 360 degree appraisal? The open organisation should not insist that people take part, nor can it pressure people unreasonably. The best way to ensure that people take part is to demonstrate that it works and that it is fair. If people do not want to take part then accept this. Then implement the system and, if the system works well, these employees are likely to want to opt in. This is a secret of the open organisation, lead by example, demonstrate what works and people will want to participate.

JOB DESCRIPTION/PERSON SPECIFICATION

The 360 degree appraisal is particularly useful when developing job descriptions and person specifications. This appraisal is still based around the individual doing the job, and still requires input from people who interact with that person. In this way a larger picture about the job is collated. The person can comment on the tasks carried out, those who interact with that person can add to that information – here they will not necessarily be discussing the performance of the par-ticular individual, but how the person doing the job will interact with them – and the appraisee and the appraiser can discuss this information during the appraisal to get the bigger picture of what is required in the job.

CONCLUDING COMMENTS

The 360 degree appraisal is becoming more popular, but organisations should be careful before implementing it. It is only appropriate where there is openness and trust, and where the employees accept the system. It is expensive to implement properly; half-hearted attempts will inevitably fail.

8

Preparation

In this chapter:

◆ **Performance criteria**

◆ **Rating scales**

◆ **Objectives**

◆ **Psychometric tests**

◆ **Choosing the right data**

◆ **The pre-appraisal report**

◆ **Preparing for the interview**

This chapter examines the kinds of data that can be used in the appraisal interview, how it should be collected, and how participants should prepare for the interview. If an appraisal is to be carried out properly it takes time to prepare. Both the appraiser and the appraisee should collect relevant information, collate it, and bring it to the appraisal interview.

It is generally the role of the appraiser to collect the information required for the appraisal – but this is not necessarily so. Much information can just as easily be collected by the appraisee. Relevant information might include previous appraisals, information about courses attended and performance indicators. The appraiser may collate notes of discussions with appraisee's coworkers, customers, clients and other managers. It is helpful if there is a list of questions to consider while preparing for the appraisal. What these are will depend on the purposes of the appraisal, and what the appraiser and the appraisee wish to cover.

USING PERFORMANCE CRITERIA

Assessing performance is often important to the organisation though assessing individual performance within the context of the organisation is often very difficult, as performance may depend heavily on the effectiveness of other people, or of the organisation in its broader context. Put simply, if the organisation is not functioning effectively, it cannot expect the individual employee to function effectively. This should be borne in mind whenever you are planning to assess performance.

Performance targets should be **objective and fair**. The extent to which this ideal is attained will depend on a number of factors such as the type of job and the validity of the data. Sometimes it appears to be straightforward to establish performance criteria. A salesperson sells x number of widgets in a set period. That is the performance target. But it is rarely that simple. Even here the appraiser must take other factors into account, such as:

◆ size of sales territory;

◆ number of pre-existing customers;

◆ number of potential customers;

◆ experience in job;

◆ type of items sold;

◆ whether the country is in recession.

Once we start to examine professional jobs the situation becomes ever more complex. How do you establish performance targets for university lecturers? What does it mean to deliver a good lecture? Has the person put across the information clearly? What does that mean? The students enjoyed it? Students have to learn many things they will not enjoy, no matter how good the lecture. The lecture was peer-rated? What are the criteria on which the lecture was rated? It becomes an impossible task. It is similar for many management jobs. It is very difficult to establish fair, objective and meaningful performance criteria for managers. Should you measure the performance of a manager by the way they treat staff in their department? How do you measure this? Do you measure them by the number of tasks completed? How do you assess the value of each task? Sometimes it is possible to resolve these issues by referring to the job description, or by comparing performance with colleagues. For instance, does the appraisee take longer to complete a task to the same standard than a colleague? It is important to examine how well the manager's department performed during the year, but there are added difficulties:

- the people in the department may be more or less skilled, or more or less motivated (by factors outside the manager's control);

- external forces may govern the performance of the department;

- the workers may be the ones driving good perform-ance, carrying the manager along;

- the department may perform well because the general economy is booming.

There are so many factors involved that simple performance criteria are extremely difficult to establish for any job. But do not be disillusioned. The important thing is to establish criteria that are as effective as possible, and then to keep in mind their limitations when discussing performance issues in the appraisal. In the end the best that can be hoped for is a reasonable mix of objective and subjective performance criteria. These factors are a good argument against performance-related pay.

Important

The criteria that are chosen, whether relating to professional appraisees or others, should enable the appraiser to accurately determine whether an employee is performing efficiently. In the end, the appraiser needs to know who is performing well, who is not, and why.

There is no simple answer to the question of how to assess performance in professional jobs, but the question does need careful consideration. It is not efficient to introduce subjective judgements (easy to obtain) simply because it is difficult to find more objective data sources.

SUPERVISOR, PEER AND UPWARD RATINGS

One criterion commonly used for many types of job is supervisor ratings. Supervisors are given a questionnaire about the appraisee to complete. The supervisor is asked to rate the performance of the appraisee on a number of factors using a numerical scale. There may also be questions needing qualitative responses.

Ratings are not only collected from supervisors. Peers, people carrying out the same job as the appraisee, often have something valuable to say about the appraisee, as also do the people the appraisee supervises (often called upward ratings). The same rules as for the design of supervisor ratings largely apply, and so all are considered together here.

Potential problems with rating questionnaires

There are some complications which you need to be aware of when analysing the results of rating questionnaires. Findings may be artificially inflated or deflated according to the regard in which the appraisee is held. They may be artificially low because of rivalry or jealousy; they may be artificially inflated because colleagues do not wish to be seen in a negative light by the person who analyses the findings. Scores may be affected by personality clashes. These effects may or may not be decreased by making the scores anonymous. The distribution of scores on particular questions can be helpful. If there is consistency between scores on particular items then the score can usually be interpreted with some accuracy. There can be problems using upward ratings, both because some people may not want to criticise their supervisor, and also because they may wish to over-criticise them!

Important

The way that ratings questionnaires are completed depends a lot on the culture of the organisation. If there is openness and trust then people are more likely to complete the scale accurately.

Further problems of rating scales include:

◆ poor design;

◆ asking the wrong questions;

◆ people are not trained to complete them properly.

These are important points. Fortunately they do not mean that ratings are useless. Properly designed, they can be very effective in all sorts of situations, and the results produced can be reasonably (though never entirely) objective.

The right questions to ask

The particular questions that are used in the questionnaire depend on the:

+ nature of the job;

+ person doing the job;

+ purposes of the appraisal;

+ nature of supervision (whether given or received).

The questions should be:

+ carefully worded;

+ unambiguous;

+ not encouraging the person to respond in any particular fashion;

+ not so general as to be meaningless (eg is X a nice person?).

It is wise to obtain professional help in developing suitable rating questionnaires, though this can be an expensive option which is only viable in larger organisations. The following guidelines, if closely ob-

served, will help you design good questionnaires that
suit your own organisation.

The rating system

A five-point measure is most common, eg:

Would you consider X gets on well with his/her
colleagues?

Gets on				Gets on
very well				very badly
5	4	3	2	1

More than five points and the difference between any
two adjacent points becomes difficult to discriminate.
You could use a 4- or 6-point measure if you want to
force people to respond either positively or negatively
(there is no mid-point).

The appraiser has to make sure the person completing
the measures knows how to answer them properly.
Without training, there are big differences in the way
people use such measures. On a 5-point measure, some
people will always use the middle points, 2,3,4; and
others will always use the extremes, 1,5. You have to
ensure that people are trained to use the full range of
scores available.

You should ensure that the right questions are asked,
that the questionnaire covers all the important areas,

and that you do not ask too many questions. Remember, many people hate completing questionnaires! You should rarely have a questionnaire that is longer than one or two sides of A4. Often, five or six questions may be enough, covering areas such as:

◆ How does the person get on with colleagues/supervisors/supervisees?

◆ Do they manage effectively?

◆ Are they efficient?

◆ Do they treat people appropriately?

When you use qualitative items it is best to ensure that you do not steer people into making particular responses. Good broad questions are:

◆ Name up to three things X is good at, and explain why.

◆ Name up to three things X is not as good at, and explain why.

Behaviourally-anchored rating scales (BARS)

One way of resolving some of the problems with traditional rating questionnaires is to use BARS.

Traditional rating scales lack definition. What does it mean to score 2 or 4? It is not explicit. If judgements are, instead, based on observable behaviour, these problems can be overcome. The scale should contain a clear definition of the trait to be rated, eg friendliness. It should also have a description of the behaviours that can be observed at any level on a scale measuring that trait, eg 1 = always smiles at and speaks to colleagues, shows consideration, and enjoys social contact; 5 = a sullen person, ignores colleagues and does not get involved in social activities.

BARS are devised by determining the key aspects of job performance (from the job description), then developing 'anchors' by asking individuals to describe a number of critical incidents – key events in working life. These are then sorted and assigned to each of the key aspects of job performance. The incidents are then scaled and a rating scale is produced for each of the key aspects of job performance. The major problem with BARS is that they are highly job specific and expensive to produce (generic BARS are available for personal characteristics, and may be useful), but they are more reliable and valid than normal rating scales.

An example of a supervisor rating questionnaire is given in Figure 4.

Please complete the following questionnaire with regard to the performance of [appraisee]. Please ensure you use the rating scale carefully, as you have been trained.

Return the questionnaire to [appraiser] by [date].

How would you describe your relationship with [appraisee]?

Very friendly	1
Friendly	2
Cordial	3
Rather strained	4
Very difficult	5

Would you say [appraisee] fits in well with colleagues?

Very well integrated into team	1
Reasonably well integrated into team	2
There are sometimes problems between [appraisee] and colleagues	3
There are often problems between [appraisee] and colleagues	4

If you responded 3 or 4, please explain why.

Does [appraisee] generally have good relations with his/her customers and other contacts outside the organisation?

very good				very poor
1	2	3	4	5

If you answered 4 or 5, please indicate why

When [appraisee] has a problem with work, does he/she approach you or some other appropriate person for help?

Never   sometimes   usually   always

Which statement best describes [appraisee] regarding the job?

Very knowledgeable, keeps up-to-date on all developments	1
Very knowledgeable about most areas of work	2
Reasonably knowledgeable	3
There are some areas of weakness	4
Not very knowledgeable about many aspects of work	5

Is the overall standard of [appraisee's] work:

Very good	1
Good	2
Average	3
Below average	4
Poor	5

If you answered 4 or 5, please indicate why.

Please comment on any particular strengths or weakness in [appraisee's] work.

Please comment on [appraisee's] overall performance.

Figure 4. Example of a supervisor rating questionnaire.

Important

Never just use rating questionnaires, BARS or otherwise, on their own. Always use the results with the appraisee as a discussion issue.

PERFORMANCE AGAINST PREVIOUS OBJECTIVES

Targets set at previous appraisals should be included as part of the pre-appraisal report. They should be clearly related to actual performance so both parties understand the general level of performance, the successes and failures, at a glance. Previously set objectives will be clearly indicated on the last appraisal report.

It is helpful to review previous objectives when setting new ones. At a glance you can see where the appraisee is strong and where they are weaker.

Assessing targets

Targets for a salesperson might include total number of sales, number of customers, number of repeat customers, plus whatever else is deemed important. These numerical figures can be put side by side with actual performance, so success and failures are immediately clear – bearing in mind the discussion earlier about the limitations of *any* numerical criteria. If the appraisee has failed to meet any particular target, for example the target for new customers, then the reasons for this can be discussed at the appraisal. Perhaps they were so busy with repeat customers that there was not time to establish many new contacts, or few of the people approached actually bought goods. Whatever the reasons, the areas for discussion are obvious at a glance. An example of a simple form comparing targets with actual performance is provided in Figure 5.

Appraisee's name:

Appraiser's name:

Date:

	Target	Actual
Number of customers (N)		
Total value of sales (£)		
Average value of sale per customer (£/N)		
Number of new contacts (Co)		
Number of new customers (Cu)		
Proportion of contacts turned into customers (Cu/Co)		
Size of territory (T)		
Sales per size of territory (£/T)		
Estimated number of potential customers		

Figure 5. Objectives and actual performance: sales personnel.

Assessing performance

Areas of effective and less effective performance are readily determined, showing which areas need to be discussed at the appraisal. Using a form similar to Figure 5 will generate certain questions which are more sophisticated than simple sales figures. Why is the value of sales per customer so low? Is the appraisee spreading themselves too thin? Why are so few new contacts turned into customers? Is the appraisee asking the wrong people?

Targets for a team can be determined by looking at overall performance, examining sales territories, discussing possibilities with the team and creating mutually acceptable targets.

PSYCHOMETRIC MEASURES

Formal psychological measures are not usually used in an appraisal situation, though they might be useful in certain circumstances, particularly where there is the possibility of retraining for another role, transfer or promotion. Psychometric tests can provide excellent information to use in the discussions. There is a wide range of psychometric tests, including:

- general intelligence;

- specific abilities (eg numerical, verbal);

- aptitudes (suitability for particular jobs);

- personality;

- team working;

- interests;

- motivation.

Not all of these will be useful in the appraisal situation. You might want to use interest and aptitude measures when considering transfer and promotion. You might want to employ team-working measures when you are looking at the performance of the team as a whole, perhaps with a view to training.

Psychometric measures should be used appropriately. Many are protected and can only be used by a qualified person, either a psychologist or someone trained in the use of specific measures. The British Psychological Society (BPS) publishes a list of Chartered Psychologists. This should be available in local libraries. The address for the BPS is in Further Reading at the end of the book.

The range of measures available can be bewildering (another good reason why you should employ someone to provide advice). The following provides some brief advice about the kinds of measures available. As you will see from the examples, some of the questions do not obviously measure what they claim to measure!

Ability tests

These include general ability (or IQ) tests, which demonstrate broad general levels of intelligence. More details about specific abilities, eg verbal, numerical, spatial, can be obtained by employing tests specifically designed for these purposes.

Examples:

- What is the next number in the series 1 3 7 15 31?

- Which is the odd one out: biron, porwsra, yenha, gelae?

- In each row of words, find the word which means the same or the opposite as the first word in the row:

many:	ill few down sour
ancient:	dry long happy old

Aptitude tests

These are designed to measure suitability for particular jobs, eg sales, mechanical or supervisory roles.

Examples:

*(Sales) Read the following statements. Mark the one that is most like you with an **M**, mark the one that is least like you with an **L**.

My selling is highly personal

I am a conservative dresser

I sometimes make price concessions to close a sale

I have a good feel for people's reactions.

*(Clerical) Coding   Plastic   25

                      Rubber   12

                      China   18

Mark the correct response: Rubber   25   12   18

                                    Plastic   25   12   18

                                    China   25   12   18

Personality questionnaires

These provide information about individual character-istics that can be matched to the person specification. They are particularly useful for assessing the ap-praisee's relationships with others and generating ques-tionnaires about these relationships and the appraisee's approaches to work and colleagues. For instance, perseverance and patience are needed by scientists, managers need to have leadership qualities and sales staff may need to be extroverted.

There is the danger that this kind of test can be faked by individuals to put themselves across in a more favourable light. This can be partly offset in the design of the questionnaire, but the effect of faking cannot be fully dismissed, and information from personality questionnaires should always be used in conjunction with discussions.

Teamworking measures are used to establish the kinds of team roles that people are most effective in. Some people are better at leading, some are better at presenting ideas, some prefer to be contentious and argumentative, some are individualistic, some are good at getting the job finished. A good team will have a range of people in these different team roles.

Examples:
*I find myself at the centre of attention at parties
    usually   sometimes   never
*People talk to me about their personal problems
    usually   sometimes   never

Interest/values questionnaires

These help reveal an individual's basic interests and attitudes across a wide area. How suitable is the individual for a particular job? What other kinds of activities might they be interested in?

Examples:
*Which job would you prefer?

Firefighter

Banker

*Mark the statement that is most (M) like you and least (L) like you:

To have a hot meal at night

To get a good night's sleep

To get plenty of fresh air.

Motivation questionnaires

These help determine what it is that motivates people, what drives them to act in the ways they do. Some basic motivators include: family, job satisfaction, money, self-worth.

Examples:

*True wisdom comes through knowing yourself:

very true   true   false   very false

*Which of the following is the least reliable sign of success in a person's career?

Position of seniority

Rate of promotion

Reputation in the trade or profession

Salary.

Which measure?

Circumstances will dictate which particular measures are most appropriate. For most appraisals, psychometric measures will be unnecessary. The choice of measure will depend on factors such as the nature of the appraisal, the type of job and the resources of the organisation.

CHOOSING WHICH DATA TO COLLECT

This depends on the type of appraisal that is being carried out.

Importance of current data

It is essential that any job within the organisation has a current job description and person specification.

Having a current job description ensures that the organisation is efficiently staffed, there are the right number of employees, they are in the right jobs, and that the jobs are clearly defined. These documents should always be available to the appraiser so they are knowledgeable about the requirements of the job and the person doing the job. The documents are key sources of data when the appraisal is concerned with staff movement, whether transfer or promotion, and when training needs are being assessed.

Of course, the regular appraisal will not normally need to examine the job description or person specification in any depth. But it is important that it is there. The person specification can be helpful if there are issues relating to performance. Compare the individual doing the job with the explicit person specification and check for discrepancies. If the specification is accurate (and it should be), and the details of performance you have for the individual are accurate and complete (and they should be) then you should be able to identify where the problem lies; and then decide on an appropriate course of action.

THE PRE-APPRAISAL REPORT

Once all the relevant information has been collected it should be condensed and put together in a standard format – usually one or more pages of text, bullet points and perhaps tables. Both parties should have a copy of this before the interview. It is important that you both work to the same report. There should be no hidden agenda.

The construction of the pre-appraisal report can be the responsibility of one or other of the parties, depending on the purpose of the appraisal. Performance measures, rating scale analyses, and any other formal documentation should normally be collated by the appraiser. As the agenda of the appraisal itself will to a large extent depend on the content of the pre-appraisal report, it is important that the appraisee has a chance to make a significant input to it.

If there are supervisor, peer, or upward ratings then it is best if the raw data is not seen by either party. The analyses should be carried out outside the department, perhaps by human resources, or by an external consultant. This will avoid the identification of individuals.

Keeping it simple

The report should be concise and intelligible. It should not be too long. Everyone is busy and the appraisal should not become too onerous. While what has been said in the last few chapters may make it appear that the appraisal is going to take up a lot of time, that should not normally be the case. The pre-appraisal report should contain the summary analyses of any measures taken, the performance indices, and details of the issues the appraisee and the appraiser wish to raise. If there is a need for some more detailed analyses relating to any of these, then they can be raised as appropriate. If they are not necessary, do not bother with them – as long as they are available to both parties should that become necessary.

It is helpful if the pre-appraisal report has a number of headings or questions to help with completion. Figure 6 provides an example of a pre-appraisal form. The purpose of such a form is to help collate the appropriate information. While it is aimed at the appraisee, both the appraiser and the appraisee may need to supply information. The actual content will vary considerably between types of organisation.

This form is designed to help facilitate a discussion between you and your appraiser. It focuses on your performance, on your training and development needs, and your aspirations, all taking into account the plans of the organisation. The appraisal will help you to take appropriate action to realise your potential and help us to recognise the contributions you have made to the organisation.

The purpose of the appraisal is to provide you with a forum to speak openly and freely about the issues that are important to you.

We would appreciate you also completing the job description attached to the form, indicating your own views of your job and the tasks it entails. Please feel free to attach any further information you think is appropriate relating to the issues you would like to discuss.

Please note that the appraisal is confidential between yourself and your appraiser. Any documents you attach may not be seen by a third party without your explicit agreement.

Name: Position: Staff number:
Name of appraiser: Date of appraisal:

1. (a) Achievements (please relate this to the objectives specified in your previous appraisal).

   (b) Comments on achievements (of particular interest are achievements which were not given as objectives in the previous appraisal and areas where you do not feel you have achieved your objectives).

2. The future (please comment on your expectations for the future in terms of performance, training needs, and aspirations).

Figure 6. The appraisee preparation form.

Both the appraiser and the appraisee will have copies of the appraisal form from the previous year (if appropriate) so they can base their preparations on the objectives and needs specified on that form.

The design of the form used will depend on a range of circumstances, from what the appraisal is about to who completes it. Once the purpose of the appraisal is clear, it should not be a difficult task to devise an appropriate appraisal preparation form – there is no such thing as an off-the-shelf form, though a template can help.

Preparing the ground in advance

It is important that both parties receive the report well in advance of the appraisal interview so that they have time to digest the contents and prepare their responses. It is on the basis of this report that each party decides on the specific topics they wish to discuss, or the specific questions they wish to ask in the interview. This works both ways. The process is not an interrogation (though some appraisers might prefer it that way!).

Keeping a flexible agenda

Appraisees may wish to raise issues that are not strictly 'on the agenda'; that do not relate to the purposes of the appraisal as outlined at the outset. They should not be deterred from raising issues that are not on the agenda. The appraisal is their opportunity to discuss exactly what they think about the organisation. Because some issues may arise for which the appraiser may not have an answer, it is appropriate for them to defer a response until they can obtain the relevant information.

UNDERSTANDING YOUR OPPOSITE NUMBER

Before an effective appraisal interview can take place, it should be ensured that:

◆ Each party understands the purposes of the appraisal.

◆ Each party has a copy of the pre-appraisal report and has understood the contents.

◆ Both parties know what issues they want to raise.

Once this has been prepared, and it is not as difficult as it might sometimes appear, then each party will understand what the other wants to get out of the appraisal. This is particularly important for the appraisee – it is their interview. The appraisal should be seen not to be something to look forward to with foreboding, but as an opportunity. Nervousness about an interview – any type of interview – arises partly out of ignorance about what will happen in the interview. There should be no big suprises – certainly not for the appraisee.

If the report for a member of sales staff contains information about sales performance, and they have failed to reach their targets, you would doubtless want to raise this in the interview. If the appraisee is aware of this then they have an opportunity to prepare their reasons why the targets were not met. The interview is not a place to put the appraisee on the spot, it is to help them. The appraisee should have ample opportunity to think about the issues you wish to raise.

PREPARING FOR THE INTERVIEW

The interview itself should follow a pre-determined agenda. Some appraisers may see this as an unnecessary chore, but it is vital. Rambling, unfocused interviews generally fail to provide the information required. They may amount to little more than informal chats with no direction or purpose. But for the appraiser who has got this far through this book, who has determined the purposes of the appraisal, discussed this with the appraisee, obtained appropriate information, and compiled a report, it would be unwise not to consider the plan of the interview itself.

The interview should consist of a number of stages, depending on the type of appraisal and the number and type of discussion points. Both parties should be well prepared for the interview, knowing exactly what is going to be discussed (with some flexibility for the appraisee), so it should largely be a matter of deciding the order of the points. The general plan should be like this:

1. The appraisal is usually different from the selection interview in that both parties usually know each other, often very well, so the first stage of setting someone at their ease will be different. It is still necessary to put the appraisee at their ease, to help them relax, as many people are nervous about appraisals.

2. Discuss any points arising from the report. Cover these fully. It is crucial to allow the appraisee full opportunity to raise any relevant issues that they see as important. You will probably integrate performance and training issues, as one may arise from the other. Ensure you stay focused.

3. Summarise the findings of the report and the discussion. Ensure that the appraisee agrees with this summary. This is important to ensure that both parties are on the same wavelength!

4. Draw conclusions from the appraisal. This may involve everything from setting performance targets to determining training needs. These should be mutually satisfactory. It is always best if the appraisee agrees the performance targets, and you agree with training needs.

Within this framework, the discussion of particular topics can be arranged in any sensible order, but do not lose sight of the fact that the interview is a conversation between two individuals with needs to be addressed, it should remain focused and – importantly – it should recognise that people have different styles of working, which should be acknowledged.

$$\bigcirc 9$$

Conducting the interview

In this chapter:

- ◆ The interview should take place at a time convenient to both parties.

- ◆ There should be adequate time set aside for the appraisal.

- ◆ The setting for the appraisal should be comfortable, and there should be no interruptions.

- ◆ There should be a clear plan for the appraisal, which should be followed.

- ◆ The appraisal report can be completed by either party, and should contain details of what was agreed in the appraisal.

PREPARING FOR THE INTERVIEW

At this stage, the participants in the appraisal should have completed:

do not try to put it into any break, it is a work task. If the interview is too rushed the parties may be unable to cover all the points they wish to raise, and important issues may be rushed over or ignored altogether. In this case the appraisee may come away frustrated because of the lack of time to discuss an important point. This could be seriously demotivating.

The length of the interview will depend on what has to be covered but, apart from the most basic appraisal, few sessions last less than one hour. Many last two hours. If the interview lasts much longer than this then the parties will lose concentration. Ensure that the length of time is appropriate for purpose. If in doubt, allow what you think will be too much time, but do not let the interview go on too long.

CHOOSING THE PLACE FOR THE INTERVIEW

The interview should take place in a quiet, warm, and well-ventilated room, with comfortable chairs and drinks (not alcohol!) available. Avoid interruptions by visitors or telephones. The image of the appraiser sitting behind a big desk and the appraisee cowering in front of it on a lower chair should be avoided. Confrontation does not help communication. The appraisee should not feel cowed, nor should the appraiser exploit any power situation. The best position is sitting roughly at right angles to each other

- ◆ setting the purposes of the appraisal;

- ◆ collecting appropriate information;

- ◆ disseminating the information via the pre-appraisal report;

- ◆ clarifying the agenda for the meeting.

This chapter focuses on the appraisal interview itself. When and where should the interview take place? What questions should be asked? How should the report be discussed and compiled? There are a range of interview skills which help in the smooth running of the interview, such as the right kinds of questions to ask, non-verbal communication such as making eye contact, and making seating arrangements.

INTERVIEW SCHEDULING

There are a number of guidelines for carrying out interviews.

Advance warning

The timing of the interview should be set well in advance (ie several weeks) so that both parties can fit their other work around the appraisal, and there are no clashes with other appointments. It is normally the responsibility of the appraiser to organise this. Adequate notice will allow enough time for both parties to prepare for the appraisal. It is important that appraisees recognise the importance of the appraisal in their work schedule, that it is perceived to be useful and not just a chore that interferes with their 'real work'. This is of course the responsibility of the organisation. If the organisation takes the appraisal seriously and genuinely responds to the outcomes of appraisal interviews then the system will work. The appraisal is part of the effective functioning of an organisation – but only if the organisation itself is functioning effectively.

Do ensure that there is adequate time before the interview to prepare properly. Complex facts and figures may not be found in a few days. If a job description has to be devised, it will take weeks. On the other hand, the time span should not be too long. It is of little value to have the appraisee thinking about an annual appraisal for months. It may affect their job performance. Appraisal should be a psychologically demanding exercise for the appraisee, but it should not take over. Systematic preparation of the kind already described should minimise the stress, so there is little point increasing it again by giving the appraisee too long to think about the appraisal.

Picking the right time

If possible, the meeting should be arranged for a time (of day, week, month or year) when the appraisee is not likely to be too busy. Many jobs have busy and less busy periods. To take a simplistic example, a mince pie salesman should not have a review in the few months before Christmas, the busiest time for mince pies. Neither should the appraisal take place just after Christmas, because there will not be time for the organisation to have collected the sales performance figures for the Christmas period.

Perhaps April would be a good month: after the rush, after the figures have been compiled, but before the next busy period gets underway. Other jobs have different busy periods, but the rule still applies; arrange the interview for when the appraisee is less busy, so that there will be time to carry out adequate preparation. This will help the appraisee stop worrying about work that has to be done. It will also ensure a minimum loss of productivity.

Upsetting the appraisee's normal work routine should be avoided as much as possible, but is should be emphasised that, in the end, the appraisal *is* part of the normal work routine.

Deciding how long the interview should be

The interview needs to have a long enough time slot. Do not try to cram it into a half hour lunch break –

perhaps with a low table nearby to put papers and drinks on.

CONDUCTING THE INTERVIEW

Both parties should ensure they bring along a copy of the pre-appraisal report, marked with any parts they wish to discuss. It is not enough to rely on memory to recall the points one wishes to raise. Both should also have paper and a pen to jot down anything of importance during the appraisal.

The actual structure of the interview will vary as people favour different approaches, and the purposes of the interview are different. What follows are some general guidelines.

The structure of the interview

The interview could start with a short informal chat on general topics not related to the interview, just to ensure both parties are relaxed. Then discuss points arising from the pre-appraisal report. Follow the structure of the report to provide focus and to ensure that all points are covered. This will be the main part of the appraisal, as all major topics should have been mentioned on the pre-appraisal report, including discussing performance, strengths and weaknesses, opportunities and problems, achievements and under-achievements, ideas for change, future objectives, and a consideration of training and other matters. The discussion should thoroughly cover the points raised, as through discussion clarity will be achieved.

Points to bear in mind

Certain things should be kept in mind during the interview:

◆ The purposes of the appraisal. The review should not stray from the pre-determined purposes. It is a simple trap to fall into. One thing leads to another, and you start to discuss a potential opening in another department; neither of you are prepared. The appraiser does not know all the details of the post, and the appraisee has not had a chance to prepare an argument for why they would be good for the post. If this happens, you may be able to cover the point adequately, but if not you may need to plan another meeting to discuss the position, particularly if the outcome may have an important impact on the appraisee's role. The responsibility for keeping the interview focused is the appraiser's.

◆ The interview should progress at a sensible rate and cover the issues it is meant to cover. You do need to spend enough time on topics, but there can be a danger of labouring a point and failing to progress. The appraiser should keep control and move on appropriately. This is a skill that can take time to learn. Think about how long you have got, how many points you have to cover, their relative importance and, at the start of the meeting, provide a rough allocation of time to each and try to keep to this.

◆ Notes should be made by both parties throughout. These will form the basis for the final report. Both of you should jot down points discussed, agreements reached and action to be taken. It is also important to note where agreement could not be reached.

◆ A record should be made of the appraisee's agreed performance objectives for the coming period. It is essential to avoid confusion here. The objectives should be clearly laid out, translated into sensible performance criteria (so they can be assessed later), unambiguous and (crucially) achievable. Remember, it is often the appraisee who is too ambitious regarding what they can achieve.

Communicating with the appraisee

There may be points on which the two parties cannot agree. If this is on performance objectives, an area where in the end there has to be agreement, then there should be the potential for recourse to someone who has the capacity to act as adjudicator, who can make the final decision based on the evidence provided by both the appraiser and the appraisee. This is best avoided but can be necessary. The appraiser should not normally be the final arbitrator. If the appraiser has the final power of imposing objectives then the bargaining power of the appraisee is diminished from the start. The appraisee may lose confidence and trust in the appraisal system. It is of course not always possible to avoid imposing objectives, and if this is the case then it is necessary; but be aware that the appraisee may be demotivated if they feel that they do not have autonomy to make their own decisions. Demotivation can mean reduced productivity and discontent.

Proposing action

The appraiser may be in a position to propose action to be taken, such as training, but they may not always be in a position to authorise such action without referral to management. The appraiser should never make promises they cannot keep. If an action has to be authorised elsewhere say so. The appraiser should make it clear that they will recommend a course of action, but that the final decision will be made by a third person.

Praise and criticism

The appraiser should bear in mind the importance of both praise and constructive criticism. During the perhaps with a low table nearby to put papers and drinks on.

CONDUCTING THE INTERVIEW

Both parties should ensure they bring along a copy of the pre-appraisal report, marked with any parts they wish to discuss. It is not enough to rely on memory to recall the points one wishes to raise. Both should also have paper and a pen to jot down anything of importance during the appraisal.

The actual structure of the interview will vary as people favour different approaches, and the purposes of the interview are different. What follows are some general guidelines.

The structure of the interview

The interview could start with a short informal chat on general topics not related to the interview, just to ensure both parties are relaxed. Then discuss points arising from the pre-appraisal report. Follow the structure of the report to provide focus and to ensure that all points are covered. This will be the main part of the appraisal, as all major topics should have been mentioned on the pre-appraisal report, including discussing performance, strengths and weaknesses, opportunities and problems, achievements and under-achievements, ideas for change, future objectives, and a consideration of training and other matters. The discussion should thoroughly cover the points raised, as through discussion clarity will be achieved.

Points to bear in mind

Certain things should be kept in mind during the interview:

◆ The purposes of the appraisal. The review should not stray from the pre-determined purposes. It is a simple trap to fall into. One thing leads to another, and you start to discuss a potential opening in another department; neither of you are prepared. The appraiser does not know all the details of the post, and the appraisee has not had a chance to prepare an argument for why they would be good for the post. If this happens, you may be able to cover the point adequately, but if not you may need to plan another meeting to discuss the position, particularly if the outcome may have an important impact on the appraisee's role. The responsibility for keeping the interview focused is the appraiser's.

◆ The interview should progress at a sensible rate and cover the issues it is meant to cover. You do need to spend enough time on topics, but there can be a danger of labouring a point and failing to progress. The appraiser should keep control and move on the final decision based on the evidence provided by both the appraiser and the appraisee. This is best avoided but can be necessary. The appraiser should not normally be the final arbitrator. If the appraiser has the final power of imposing objectives then the bargaining power of the appraisee is diminished from the start. The appraisee may lose confidence and trust in the appraisal system. It is of course not always possible to avoid imposing objectives, and if this is the case then it is necessary; but be aware that the appraisee may be demotivated if they feel that they do not have autonomy to make their own decisions. Demotivation can mean reduced productivity and discontent.

Proposing action

The appraiser may be in a position to propose action to be taken, such as training, but they may not always be in a position to authorise such action without referral to management. The appraiser should never make promises they cannot keep. If an action has to be authorised elsewhere say so. The appraiser should make it clear that they will recommend a course of action, but that the final decision will be made by a third person.

Praise and criticism

The appraiser should bear in mind the importance of both praise and constructive criticism. During the appropriately. This is a skill that can take time to learn. Think about how long you have got, how many points you have to cover, their relative importance and, at the start of the meeting, provide a rough allocation of time to each and try to keep to this.

◆ Notes should be made by both parties throughout. These will form the basis for the final report. Both of you should jot down points discussed, agreements reached and action to be taken. It is also important to note where agreement could not be reached.

◆ A record should be made of the appraisee's agreed performance objectives for the coming period. It is essential to avoid confusion here. The objectives should be clearly laid out, translated into sensible performance criteria (so they can be assessed later), unambiguous and (crucially) achievable. Remember, it is often the appraisee who is too ambitious regarding what they can achieve.

Communicating with the appraisee

There may be points on which the two parties cannot agree. If this is on performance objectives, an area where in the end there has to be agreement, then there should be the potential for recourse to someone who has the capacity to act as adjudicator, who can make discussion, whenever it is shown that the appraisee has done something praiseworthy, then use praise. It is a great motivator. On the other hand when the appraisee has failed to do something well, this should also be pointed out; but criticism should be constructive, it is about finding ways of helping the appraisee find a way of improving. Do not just say, 'Your performance was poor', say, 'Your performance was poor. I think it might be because of X. What do you think?' Or better still, 'Your performance was poor. Why do you think this was so?' The appraisee will accept criticism much more readily if it is constructive. If it is not supported by evidence, or if it is simply a telling off then the appraisee is likely to feel they have been unfairly treated and resent the organisation – which leads to reduced morale and productivity.

Closure

By the close of the interview, all discussion points should have been covered in a way that is acceptable to both parties. The purposes of the appraisal should have been met, conclusions agreed, such as setting objectives for the coming period or offering training. The interview should end amicably, even if the discussion became heated because of disagreement. Nothing is gained by taking anger or animosity away from the meeting.

APPRAISING UNDER-PERFORMERS AND STAFF WITH PROBLEMS

There are always going to be situations where appraisees have problems either with performance or with some other aspects of their job. In both cases it is important to deal with problems when they arise. Do not wait for the formal appraisal. It is a truism that a problem is less of a problem if it is nipped in the bud. Many issues can be resolved with a quick chat before they become problems. The appraiser should always be supportive and constructive, whatever the problem. One helpful tip is to try to look at the problem from the appraisee's perspective. Why do they think they are underperforming? What is their perception of the problem?

If the issue relates to performance then a good starting point is to review the targets set at the previous appraisal. Were they reasonable? Have other factors arisen since then that make the targets inappropriate? Never make the prior assumption that it is the appraisee's fault. Examine the evidence and draw appropriate conclusions. Try to enable the appraisee to develop appropriate solutions.

If the situation is disciplinary (and disciplinary action should be avoided whenever possible, internal sol-

◆ setting the purposes of the appraisal;

◆ collecting appropriate information;

◆ disseminating the information via the pre-appraisal report;

◆ clarifying the agenda for the meeting.

This chapter focuses on the appraisal interview itself. When and where should the interview take place? What questions should be asked? How should the report be discussed and compiled? There are a range of interview skills which help in the smooth running of the interview, such as the right kinds of questions to ask, non-verbal communication such as making eye contact, and making seating arrangements.

INTERVIEW SCHEDULING
There are a number of guidelines for carrying out interviews.

Advance warning
The timing of the interview should be set well in advance (ie several weeks) so that both parties can fit their other work around the appraisal, and there are no clashes with other appointments. It is normally the responsibility of the appraiser to organise this. Ad-

equate notice will allow enough time for both parties to prepare for the appraisal. It is important that appraisees recognise the importance of the appraisal in their work schedule, that it is perceived to be useful and not just a chore that interferes with their 'real work'. This is of course the responsibility of the organisation. If the organisation takes the appraisal seriously and genuinely responds to the outcomes of appraisal interviews then the system will work. The appraisal is part of the effective functioning of an organisation – but only if the organisation itself is functioning effectively.

Do ensure that there is adequate time before the interview to prepare properly. Complex facts and figures may not be found in a few days. If a job description has to be devised, it will take weeks. On the other hand, the time span should not be too long. It is of little value to have the appraisee thinking about an annual appraisal for months. It may affect their job performance. Appraisal should be a psychologically demanding exercise for the appraisee, but it should not take over. Systematic preparation of the kind already described should minimise the stress, so there is little point increasing it again by giving the appraisee too long to think about the appraisal.

Picking the right time

If possible, the meeting should be arranged for a time (of day, week, month or year) when the appraisee is not likely to be too busy. Many jobs have busy and less busy periods. To take a simplistic example, a mince pie salesman should not have a review in the few months before Christmas, the busiest time for mince pies. Neither should the appraisal take place just after Christmas, because there will not be time for the organisation to have collected the sales performance figures for the Christmas period.

Perhaps April would be a good month: after the rush, after the figures have been compiled, but before the next busy period gets underway. Other jobs have different busy periods, but the rule still applies; arrange the interview for when the appraisee is less busy, so that there will be time to carry out adequate preparation. This will help the appraisee stop worrying about work that has to be done. It will also ensure a minimum loss of productivity.

Upsetting the appraisee's normal work routine should be avoided as much as possible, but is should be emphasised that, in the end, the appraisal *is* part of the normal work routine.

Deciding how long the interview should be

The interview needs to have a long enough time slot. Do not try to cram it into a half hour lunch break –

do not try to put it into any break, it is a work task. If the interview is too rushed the parties may be unable to cover all the points they wish to raise, and important issues may be rushed over or ignored altogether. In this case the appraisee may come away frustrated because of the lack of time to discuss an important point. This could be seriously demotivating.

The length of the interview will depend on what has to be covered but, apart from the most basic appraisal, few sessions last less than one hour. Many last two hours. If the interview lasts much longer than this then the parties will lose concentration. Ensure that the length of time is appropriate for purpose. If in doubt, allow what you think will be too much time, but do not let the interview go on too long.

CHOOSING THE PLACE FOR THE INTERVIEW

The interview should take place in a quiet, warm, and well-ventilated room, with comfortable chairs and drinks (not alcohol!) available. Avoid interruptions by visitors or telephones. The image of the appraiser sitting behind a big desk and the appraisee cowering in front of it on a lower chair should be avoided. Confrontation does not help communication. The appraisee should not feel cowed, nor should the appraiser exploit any power situation. The best position is sitting roughly at right angles to each other, utions are usually better) then ensure you follow appropriate procedures.

AFTER THE INTERVIEW

Once the interview has been completed, details should be recorded on the appraisal form. This should be done as soon as possible after the interview, when the details are fresh to both the appraiser and the appraisee. The report should contain details of:

◆ the purposes of the interview;

◆ performance against previous objectives;

◆ points discussed;

◆ conclusions reached;

◆ objectives set;

◆ matters which remain unresolved.

While either party may complete the appraisal form, it is important to ensure that agreement is reached. The completed form should be given to the other party. If there is agreement then the form should be signed by both the appraiser and the appraisee, and copies kept by each. The completed form should be considered as confidential, and no details given to other parties except where necessary and then only by agreement with the appraisee.

The appraiser should ensure that action points are acted on as appropriate. If immediate training needs have been identified then they should be met as soon as possible. Whether it is the appraiser or the appraisee that sorts this out will depend on the organisation, but once agreed in the appraisal it must be recognised that authority for such training has been given, unless it was clear in the interview that the appraiser could not provide the authority. In these cases the appraiser should obtain the authority as soon as practical.

Important

Providing training/development for the appraisee as agreed in the appraisal is critical to the success of the system. Too many organisations pay lip service to appraisal; promising the world and providing nothing.

The structure of the report will depend on the job. For many jobs, objectives can be quantified, so numerical scales may be appropriate. This will help immediately identify strengths and weaknesses relating to perform-ance. Do not use such scales where the performance objectives are not quantifiable. This can be misleading.

Appraisal form

This is to be completed by the appraiser, and agreed with the appraisee. If there are points of disagreement these should be resolved by discussion. If they cannot be resolved then there should be an indication of where there is disagreement.

1. **Priorities for the future.** You should discuss the appraisee's priorities and expectations, both in terms of their personal needs and in terms of performance. Please conclude this with a series of achievable and agreed objectives.

2. **Action.** Please note any actions that should be taken, including training and development needs, by whom they should be taken, and by what date.

3. **Performance.** Please comment on the appraisee's performance with regard to their previously specified objectives.

4. **Broader context.** Please comment on any aspects of the appraisal which has broader implications for the department/organisation.

We have agreed the above comments:

Signed (appraiser)

Signed (appraisee)

Date

If anything has not been agreed, please note both points of view and sign below.

Figure 7. The appraisal form.

Figure 7 provides an example of an appraisal form for completion by the appraiser immediately after the appraisal. It will contain information from both the preparatory activities carried out before the appraisal, including the pre-appraisal form completed by the appraisee (see Figure 4), the information obtained by the appraiser before the interview, and the results of the discussion in the interview itself.

Resolution of conflict

Inevitably there will be occasions where the appraiser and the appraisee disagree. These points of disagreement should be thoroughly discussed during the interview. If there remains a problem then the points of contention should be clearly identified on the appraisal form, and both parties should sign the document with this included. Where necessary, disagreements should be referred to another authority for resolution. This may involve the appraisee's line manager, human resources, or other parties as appropriate. There should be a clear procedure for these problems, so that the appraisee, if they feel aggrieved, can see that the process is fair and is being used appropriately. Conflicts should be resolved as quickly as possible to the satisfaction of both parties.

Value of the report for future reference

The appraisal report will be used for reference in future appraisals, and will help the appraisee keep track of their development in the organisation. It is also helpful if someone new is appraising the individual; the issue of confidentiality means that permission from the appraisee must be obtained before the new appraiser has access to the document.

Sometimes appraisees will not be happy about using previous reports. It may be that their performance was poor in the past, or that they feel that a previous appraiser was biased against them. This might lead to a new appraiser forming inappropriate views before the appraisal. It can in these circumstances be best to start with a clean sheet.

Job description

If the appraisal has considered the job description as described in Chapter Five then the information arising from this is, of course, not confidential. Information regarding new tasks, changes in tasks, and the recognition of changes to the person specification, should be forwarded to the human resources department so they can integrate the information appropriately.

CASE STUDY

Donna's employers misjudge the timing

Donna has been called for her appraisal interview at a particularly busy time. She has received a number of unexpected orders and is under pressure to complete them quickly. On top of the normal pressures associated with rush orders, the shop floor staff are creating difficulties regarding their overtime pay and bonus scheme. They want the bonus to be set at a higher rate than usual to compensate for the extra work and overtime involved.

Donna, understandably, does not want her appraisal at this time. She would prefer to wait a few weeks until things have calmed down, but 'the powers that be' have set the date and the time and they will not alter it.

In many ways the appraisal system of Donna's organisation is a good one. It is standardised across the organisation to ensure fair comparisons between individuals in different departments, and management appraisals are carried out by trained staff from human resources. Unfortunately there are drawbacks. The system is very rigid and does not allow for situations like Donna's, when someone is unexpectedly busy. The appraisal system has its own schedules and postponing interviews is seen as a problem to be avoided if at all possible.

Because Donna is under such pressure, her appraisal does not go well. She is ill-prepared, and the discussion fails to achieve anything significant. Targets cannot be set, as Donna is not in a position to comment on them. She wanted to discuss her future, as she is hoping for a promotion, but again this proves to be impossible because her mind is on the problems in her department. Finally the appraiser has to agree to a new interview at a more convenient time for Donna, so a lot of time has been wasted, both Donna's and the appraiser's.

Comment

The problem here is one of inflexibility. The human resources department has set up a very good appraisal system, which attempts to be fair across the whole organisation; but it lacks flexibility. The human resources department has to consider the position of people working with customers. The customer's needs have to take priority over the administration of the appraisal system. It is right that appraisals should take place at set times, but there also has to be flexibility to ensure that in emergencies the appraisal can be set back a few weeks. It is not difficult to speak to Donna and find out when she is available for the appraisal.

10

Evaluation

In this chapter:

◆ **Follow up**

◆ **Validation**

◆ **Fairness**

◆ **Identifying sources of conflict**

This chapter is concerned with how the appraisal should be followed up, and also examines ways of validating the system. There is no point in having a system that is glossy and expensive but does not work, and appraisals which do not work usually have problems concerning following through promises made to appraisees, leading to disillusionment with the system. An appraisal system should be continually monitored and evaluated, and adjusted to ensure it runs effectively.

It is important to:

+ quickly follow up recommendations for action (eg training needs);

+ ensure the appraisal system is valid and appropriate;

+ avoid unfairness, bias and sources of conflict;

+ optimise job satisfaction and organisational efficiency.

An efficient appraisal does not end with the interview. The recommendations arising from the interview must be followed up. If the appraisal recognises a training need then this should be met. The appraisal system itself should be continually monitored to ensure it is working effectively. The appraisal system can easily be unfair – or perceived as unfair, which has similar effects – if it is not monitored. That does not mean it should be continually changed to keep up with the latest ideas – not all the latest ideas are good! An appraisal system should run for several years before significant change, to ensure that participants have a chance to iron out any difficulties. One of the problems with many organisations is that innovation is considered a good thing in itself. The reality is that innovation can be extremely damaging if introduced just for its own sake.

FOLLOWING UP

Any recommendations for action that have been made in the appraisal must be followed up.

If the appraisal identifies training needs then these needs should be met as soon as practical.

There is little point in identifying an immediate training need and then not providing the training for 12 months. How can the individual be expected to perform if they do not have the opportunity to develop their skills? It might save the cost of the training course but it is potentially 12 months' extra productivity lost, and that productivity is likely to be worth much more than the cost of the training. There is also the danger of demotivating the employee by recognising a training need and then failing to provide it.

Providing appropriate training is particularly important in jobs where there is rapidly changing technology. For instance, a computer programmer will need regular training to keep up-to-date with the latest programming languages and development. It is widely acknowledged that an organisation which fails to keep up with changes in technology is likely to be unsuccessful – but there is little point in keeping up with technology if your employees do not receive appropriate training. Appraisal will help ensure that training keeps pace with changes in technology.

Making recommendations

If the appraiser is only able to *recommend* training rather than authorise it, then the appraiser should make sure they put forward the recommendations quickly, to ensure that the organisation can set up the training quickly. If for some reason the organisation refuses to authorise the training, then the appraisee should be told immediately, and provided with the reasons why the training is not forthcoming. They can then appeal against this if they feel it is appropriate. After all, the decision to recommend training will have been based on a detailed discussion during the appraisal, so the organisation will need to have very good reasons why they should not receive that training.

It is often the case that funds are not available. If this is the case let the appraisee know. It is better to say that there is no money available for training than to say nothing, and effectively let the employee know that the organisation does not value them. As mentioned above, appropriate training should be funded because in the end it will benefit the organisation through better productivity, but this is not an argument for the present book.

Keeping records

Depending on the type of job, it may be appropriate to keep continuous records of whether performance targets are being met. These records might be weekly, monthly or quarterly. These records will help encourage appraisees to achieve their targets, and will provide a useful account for the next appraisal. Regular record keeping will highlight problems quickly, which can then be addressed, rather than waiting for the next formal appraisal. This is an example of how appraisal is a continuous process.

For many jobs, it is difficult to keep appropriate records because performance is not quantifiable, and can only be assessed through discussion and analysis. In these cases it is still important to keep an eye on things, to have a regular chat with the employee to ensure that progress is satisfactory.

The importance of follow up
By following up all the recommendations of the appraisal, the organisation is showing the employee that they are important. The appraisal should show this, by not only assessing performance against objectives, but also assessing individual needs – for instance ensuring the work-home balance is met – and providing for these needs.

It is essential that there is continuity for the individual and for the organisation through the appraisal system. The appraisal is an integral part of the appraisee's working life, and it should show how the person has developed during their time with the organisation.

VALIDATING THE APPRAISAL SYSTEM

Once an appraisal system has been designed and implemented, it should not just be used when needed and never examined to check whether it is working properly. A car will develop faults if it does not receive a regular service. It is the same with appraisal. Over time it becomes outdated, and new elements need to be introduced. There are changes in jobs, changes in people and new ways of doing things. This is why your appraisal system needs to be validated.

The same basic system should be used throughout the organisation so comparisons can be made across departments. This does not mean that all appraisals will be the same. Objective measurement of objectives on the shop floor is not possible in the boardroom. Appraisals have different purposes at different times. Individuals are not the same. They each bring their own idiosyncrasies to the system – the biggest mistake any manager can make is to try to make people conform to a system without allowing for individuality. This applies more in some jobs than others. In a university it is daft to think that lecturers can be told to work to a rigid system, because lecturers are selected on the basis of individuality, not conformity; but at the same time, these lecturers will work to an outline system. The point is that the system must be practical for the people involved, and not too rigid. The point made in the case study in the previous chapter illustrates this. A rigid system will undermine the autonomy of the individual and reduce motivation.

Appraisals should be carried out efficiently, and the conclusions they draw should be useful to both the individual employee and the organisation. They should not take up too much time, but they should be taken seriously.

Objectives should be attainable, the right person chosen for training, the right person promoted, the individual enabled to be satisfied with the job.

The only way to ensure this is to regularly validate the appraisal system, to see what is working properly, to see what – if anything – should be changed, where improvements can be made.

Validation is an ongoing process set up at the same time, and as part of, the appraisal system. It will help remove teething problems with the system. Regular validation will help ensure the system runs smoothly. Over time the organisation changes; and the appraisal system should change with it. The organisation will change in size, structure, the make-up of its employees, its products, its overall philosophy. As these occur, modify the system as appropriate – but try not to throw it out, to reject it completely. Usually, for organisations at least, reform is better than revolution.

How to validate the system

The organisation should consult with employees regarding the appraisal system; how it works, where it does not work well. If the organisation does not consult with employees the system will not be accepted, and the organisation will be seen as uncaring about its staff. After all, employees are the ones who use the system, and they are likely to know best about why it works or why it does not work.

There are several ways in which the organisation can validate the system. We will consider just two here:

(a) detailed interviewing,

(b) questionnaires.

Both have their advantages and disadvantages. Interviewing is time-consuming, and there may be issues of confidentiality; but interviews are very effective. Questionnaires are faster, the organisation can obtain information from a large sample quickly, but will not provide as much depth of information.

Detailed interviewing

In order to carry out the validation, accurate records need to be kept. The records include those which are kept in the employee's personal file, along with the job descriptions and person specifications for the job. There are also the detailed records of the appraisal itself, the pre-appraisal reports, the appraisal reports, and any records of job performance.

The validation procedure can be carried out either by the human resources department or by external consultants. The latter may be better because they do not enter the process from the perspective of the organisation, and will be able to remain outside and objective.

A small number of employees should be selected who represent the range of jobs and departments within the organisations, and they are asked if they are willing to take part. Issues of confidentiality will have to be explained, as this validation requires open access to the employee's records, particularly the reports relating to the appraisal. There must be no pressure on the individual to take part. If they do agree to take part, it might be worth providing some sort of reward, as the process will be time-consuming.

The validation itself will involve the validator working through the documentation, ensuring that there is a match between the appraisal documents, that both performance objectives and training needs are being met, that recommendations are being followed through, and that the individual's career progress is acceptable, both for the person and for the organisation. Once this has been analysed the validator should interview the employee about both their own place in the organisation over the years and the appraisal system specifically. By using the appraisal reports the validator can pick up individual areas of interest and note where the appraisal may have been effective (eg providing training) or not (eg not following up recognised training needs).

Via the processes of examining the records and interviewing a number of employees the validator will be able to draw conclusions about the effectiveness of the appraisal system. They should focus on a number of areas:

- How employees perceive the system. Do they think it works? What do they think is wrong with it? What do they think works well?

- Whether the appraisal system is enabling employees to progress satisfactorily within the organisation. Whether it identifies needs and desires and tries to do something about them.

- Whether the organisation takes the appraisal system – and hence its employees – seriously.

- Potential problem areas identified in the appraisal reports. For instance recognising training needs and not following them through.

The information from the interviews should be compiled and a report on the effectiveness of the appraisal system presented, complete with any recommendations for change.

A simpler version of this method would be to ignore personnel and appraisal records, and carry out the series of depth interviews with a sample of employees. While this will not produce as much information, it does resolve the problem of confidentiality, which is likely to encourage more employees to take part.

Questionnaires

This is a simpler system to implement; it involves asking employees about their experiences of appraisal using a standardised quantitative questionnaire. It can still be carried out by either the human resources department or external consultants. Both appraisers and appraisees can be asked, and the data analysed across all participants. The questions should use a five-point rating scale:

1 = very unacceptable

2 = unacceptable

3 = barely acceptable

4 = acceptable

5 = very acceptable

The questions should relate to the range of activities relating to the appraisal, such as:

◆ the preparation of the appraiser (or appraisee);

◆ your preparation time;

◆ the pre-appraisal report;

◆ the interview itself:
  – did it cover all necessary issues in enough detail?
  – was it conducted in a professional manner?

◆ the appraisal report;

◆ adequacy of follow-up.

You may also want to include general questions about satisfaction with the review process overall, and satisfaction with the way the organisation treats its employees. Finally, you should include a general catch-all open question allowing employees space to comment on their experiences of appraisal.

The validator should analyse the information, both quantitative and qualitative, and provide an appropriate report to the organisation, with any recommendations for change.

Overview of validation

The above process should be carried out regularly, to ensure the smooth working of the appraisal system. Remember, the appraisal system should belong to the employees of the organisation. It should not be imposed on them, so introducing this kind of consultation will help ensure that employees feel that the system is theirs – which it is.

HOW APPRAISAL CAN BE UNFAIR

Unfairness and bias, inadvertent or deliberate behaviour intended to be prejudicial, can arise at any point in the appraisal system. It is essential to try to minimise this. Problems associated with the design of the appraisal system should be ironed out during the design of the system and through validation. More serious is the unfairness and bias linked to individual behaviour.

Even people who consider themselves to be extremely fair-minded and open have irrational and subjective views about other people which may be prejudicial in the work context. We cannot help being biased in our dealings with others. Often it is inadvertent; what seems fair to one person is seen as unfair by another.

Stereotyping

We create order in the social world by simplifying the information we receive about others. We interpret another person's behaviour using our prior knowledge and understanding of people. This is stereotyping. We could not function in the social world without using stereotypes. They introduce systematic bias into the way we behave with other people. Stereotyping is the process of grouping essentially heterogeneous people into homogeneous categories, such as the member of staff who is in the union is automatically labelled as a trouble-maker, even though there is no evidence for this. This is unfair, but because stereotyping is a natural human phenomenon, it is impossible to eliminate; though by recognising it, we can control it.

Unfairness arising out of stereotyping is in many cases trivial, but in some cases it can lead to serious consequences. Common stereotypes include race, gender, and social class; where a person applies a stereotype expecting certain kinds of behaviour from certain kinds of people.

First impressions

The idea of the first impression is linked to stereotypes. The first time we meet a person we automatically classify them in some way. We latch on to a particular characteristic, or look, or comment they make, and link them to our own stereotypes. Once we identify a characteristic, the person is then assumed to have the other characteristics of the stereotype.

Fortunately, the negative effects of stereotyping and first impressions can be minimised by being aware of their effects. We should not judge someone on a single comment, or on the way they look. We should remain open, allowing ourselves to change our impressions of people as we get to know them.

Example

To take a simple example, a manager may wrongly imagine that anyone with a non-standard southern English accent is lower in intelligence, tends to have less education, and has poorer leadership qualities than someone speaking received pronunciation. Though the manager may not *consciously* think in this way, they may *act* on the stereotype in the appraisal and, perhaps, fail to suggest that the appraisee is put forward for promotion. This manager is not exceptional, but is behaving in a way common to us all. We all act on **implicit assumptions**, assumptions that we have made without every knowing we have made them. This sort of thing can be avoided to a large extent when in the role of appraiser (or appraisee) by being aware of the impact of such assumptions. Ensure that decisions are reached on the basis of the evidence, including the discussion, rather than the stereotype. Awareness of stereotyping and its effects can itself reduce the negative effects because we can learn to act on the objective data rather than the subjective judgement.

Knowing people

Even when we think we know people, and we think we know their personal characteristics, their foibles, their strengths and weaknesses, we should remain open to them changing. We should not assume that people do not change. While some personality characteristics are very strong and are unlikely to ever change, people do develop and change over time, and this should be recognised.

The halo effect

Another form of unfairness is called the 'halo effect'. This occurs when the appraiser knows the appraisee has done particularly well in one area of work, and so assumes that all other areas of the job are being carried out to the same standard. The appraiser can fall into the trap of focusing on the good work, totally missing other areas where performance has been poor, or where there are particular problems. The appraisee is not likely to point these problems out.

The appraisal should not just focus on praising good work; it is important to discuss problematic areas. The appraisee does not gain by avoiding discussing any problems.

The halo effect can work in reverse. An otherwise competent individual may be over-criticised because of a single shoddy piece of work. This may lead to an unfair judgement of the individual having a reputation as a poor worker. This could then lead to a self-fulfilling prophecy. If the person is seen by others as incompetent, then this perception itself may cause them to perform incompetently.

IDENTIFYING SOURCES OF CONFLICT

No matter how open, fair and equal the appraisal system is designed to be, power games may be played between the two parties, who may often see themselves in some sort of organisation versus employee conflict. Of course, creating the open organisation can help minimise this, so a good appraisal system will depend to some extent on the structure of the organisation. Power games occur in appraisals because the roles of 'boss' and 'subordinate' may be temporarily suspended; both parties may be vying for position in their temporarily 'equal' role.

Conflict also arises from other sources:

- Within the appraisee, who may fear that the object of the appraisal is to decide who to dismiss, or who to withhold bonuses or pay rises from.

- Within the appraiser, who may believe the appraisee is trying to hide or misrepresent information.

- Within the organisation, the climate of which may foster conflict more than cooperation.

Conflict will hinder the effectiveness of the appraisal. Appraisals should be run in the fashion of the open organisation itself, in a spirit of cooperation rather than conflict, with both parties working together to solve problems.

Designers of appraisal systems need to find ways of minimising potential conflict, and one good way is via appropriate appraisal training. If both parties are aware of the potential sources of conflict, and how they harm the appraisal process, they are more likely to try to avoid them.

CASE STUDY

Conor's training needs are not followed up
Conor's appraisal was very useful, or so he thought immediately afterwards. He had discussed with Jack, his appraiser, a number

of problems he has had recently. Conor works for a car manufacturer that believes in a broad-based training for its junior managers. Following this philosophy, Conor has recently moved from production to sales to widen his experience. Unfortunately, he has found it difficult to adapt. He gets nervous when meeting new people, worrying that he is making mistakes in what he says to them. This did not matter in production, even though he was meeting people all the time. They were usually the same people. In sales it is very different. Conor has to meet people every day; and if he makes a mistake he may lose a sale.

The first three months were not very good. Conor's performance suffered. In the appraisal Jack was very sympathetic; and they both realised something needed to be done. 'Assertiveness training. That's what you need,' said Jack. Conor agreed. This was included in the appraisal report, with the comment that it needed to be provided quickly.

After the appraisal, Conor carried on as before, improving a little as time went on. He was waiting for the training, but it did not come. He contacted Jack, who said, 'I'm sorry. I had informed human resources. They should have dealt with it. I'll get on to them straightaway.' Again Conor waited and nothing happened. Again he contacted Jack, who promised to get it sorted. Eventually he received the training nine months after the appraisal, shortly before he was due to move into another role, so any benefits gained by the training would not benefit sales.

Comment

This shows how easy it is for action promised at the appraisal not to happen. The company has a very good management training programme that involves specialist training and breadth of experience, but in this instance it failed due to a lack of communication. The potential loss is significant. Apart from any ineffectiveness in Conor's performance in sales, there is a serious possibility that he will become disillusioned with the company, and either fail to live up to his potential or find a job elsewhere with a company that keeps its promises.

11

Present thoughts and future directions

In this chapter:

◆ **What is the state of appraisal?**

◆ **Work-home balance**

◆ **Legal and ethical issues**

◆ **Appraising professional and scientific staff**

◆ **The problem with staff appraisal**

This final brief chapter looks at the present and future state of staff appraisal. What is its role in organisations? This book is about improving staff appraisal, so what should we see in the future? It is essential that staff appraisal is integrated into the structure of the organisation. For staff appraisal to work effectively, the organisational climate should be conducive to trust between employer and employee.

WHAT IS THE STATE OF APPRAISAL?

Staff appraisal has many supporters and perhaps even more detractors. Some argue that it is essential to organisational effectiveness; others argue that it should be done away with as a waste of money. Unfortunately research into the effectiveness of staff appraisal is limited. There is little systematic research carried out using an appropriate scientific basis, so it is difficult to determine the true state of the area.

The vast majority of organisations use appraisal in one form or another; sometimes effectively, sometimes not. Appraisal is seen as an essential part of managing human resources. It has been estimated that over 90 per cent of organisations use appraisal, but only around 20 per cent of them have a good and fair system.

One of the biggest problems with appraisal is that it is not taken seriously, either by the employee or by the organisation. The organisation pays lip service to the appraisal and, because it does not take the needs of employees seriously, the employees themselves do not take the appraisal seriously because they know that the organisation is not really interested in their personal needs.

Appraisal cannot continue to be used as ineffectually as it currently is, nor to be perceived as poorly. The pessimistic view is that instead of paying lip-service to a poor appraisal system some organisations might as well just give it up. More optimistically, what is needed is radical change, greater openness in organisations, which would include employees having a greater voice in the running of the organisation through consultation, a flatter management structure, greater autonomy – the issues discussed in Chapter 2. A more open organisation will ideally include a fully integrated appraisal system, a system respected and acknowledged by all participants: one that works.

Integrating appraisal

The appraisal system must be fully integrated into the running of the organisation. It should never just be a once a year chat which does not achieve anything. The organisation has needs and the employee has needs. Both can be addressed in a well-planned appraisal system. Organisations have different requirements regarding appraisal; this is partly due to size, a larger organisation will need a more complex system than a smaller organisation, partly due to whether the organisation is public or private, and partly because of the people in the organisation, both managers and employees.

What I have tried to show in this book is that in order for an appraisal system to work effectively the organisation has to have a genuine interest in the well-being of its employees. This is not just so that they perform more effectively in their work, but also to recognise other needs of the individual, partly through a genuine recognition of the need to have a work-home balance, and that the rest of the employees' life, their family, leisure, etc, is at least and usually more important than their working life.

Staff appraisal is big business; but big business does not always mean good business. Care has to be taken over the design of the appraisal system, and procedures in place to validate it. In 1949 Thorndike specified four criteria for effective assessment:

- validity;

- reliability;

- freedom from bias;

- practicality.

These criteria apply to staff appraisal systems. This book has attempted to address these criteria, to help you design and implement a practical and effective appraisal system.

WORK-HOME BALANCE*

The work-home balance has taken on an increasing importance in the last few years, with both forward-thinking organisations and the Government recognising that we have to take into account the personal and individual needs of employees; that by taking these needs into account the person will have higher job satisfaction and be more productive. There are moves both nationally and internationally to reduce working hours.

Research shows that people are more productive if they work fewer hours. Clearly, if they work fewer hours more efficiently then they have more time for home and leisure activities, which will – hopefully – increase overall levels of happiness. Of course, there are exceptions. People who wish to work all their waking hours should be provided with the opportunity to do so, but those who wish to work shorter hours should not be penalised.

The organisation can examine the work-home balance through the appraisal system. It is the ideal forum for addressing non-work-related matters where they have relevance to work and where the appraisee wishes to discuss them.

---

*The term work-life balance is more usual, but work is part of life. So the distinction should be between home and work.

LEGAL AND ETHICAL ISSUES

It is important to ensure that you run a fair appraisal system, otherwise there are potential legal issues. For example, an employee could leave and claim constructive or unfair dismissal if they thought the appraisal was conducted unreasonably. Also, if the employer has a contractual appraisal system then if they fail to follow it there could be legal consequences. It is important to ensure that the system does not discriminate on grounds of race, sex, marital status, or disability.

It is important to ensure that the conversation of the interview is confidential. Many things may be said in the interview which the appraisee would not want to be known outside that situation. These may include personal or domestic issues, which may or may not impact on the job, and may or may not be relevant to the appraisal – sometimes the appraiser will have to be aware of domestic issues which might later impact on the job and can so be prepared for. These issues should certainly not be disclosed inappropriately.

APPRAISING PROFESSIONAL AND SCIENTIFIC STAFF

The difficulties

To take the example of an academic scientist, measuring performance is very difficult. The product of science is knowledge, which is difficult to quantify. Unfortunately the present political climate requires objective quantification of everything, including academic output, so academics are measured on the number of research papers they produce and the number of published pages. This criterion for performance is shown to be nonsense when we see that Einstein's original exposition of his theory of relativity was a one-page research note. It is the impact of the papers written, the contribution they make to knowledge, not the number of papers written, which matters. Unfortunately impact cannot be assessed using a tick box.

Creativity

A further problem regarding the quality of scientific output is that of creativity. Creativity does not appear to order, and it is not measurable. A scientist may spend many years apparently not achieving anything (no published papers) and then suddenly come up with an important theoretical contribution to their area. If an appraisal system had demanded particular 'objective' output through these years then perhaps the scientist would not have been allowed the intellectual space to generate the theory.

Teaching

While teachers are regularly appraised, there are serious problems with assessment at all levels of education.

The current system requires an assessment of the 'quality' of education provided; there are now league tables for everything, from the average number of examinations passed, to 'added value'; and teachers are expected to produce large quantities of written work to demonstrate how well they are doing their jobs. This information is then used in appraisal to assess performance. This is a good example of how not to assess performance. If a teacher is expected to spend hours producing written evidence of their competence then they are not spending their time teaching, and hence their 'performance' is inevitably reduced.

Performance indicators

Examples like the above can be seen in other professions. Again, there are problems associated with the measurement of performance. Should lawyers be measured on the number of cases won? Should medical doctors be measured on the number of patients cured? This is clearly absurd, though in many areas of the public sector this occurs.

This obsession with measurement should be resisted. Measurement is sometimes appropriate for appraisal purposes, but it is not relevant in many cases. There is a false argument discussed in government and business circles that in order to maximise performance we have to measure it and prove that performance is improving.

Underlying this argument is an assumption that these workers will not work effectively unless they are measured. This is unfair and inappropriate. A medical doctor will not work harder because they are being measured on the number of patients treated. They will only become increasingly exasperated because of the increasing number of forms they are expected to complete.

Professionalism

Professionals are called professionals because they have the education, training and expertise to work effectively in their chosen job. By introducing procedures which undermine their professionalism, managers of organisations are undermining loyalty; reducing job satisfaction, and hence reducing productivity. There are good arguments for allowing professionals to manage themselves, to carry out their jobs without undue interference, and hence to maximise autonomy. This is associated with the open organisations. Individuals should have the freedom to manage their own work. They will then be more productive.

The above examples show that staff appraisals for professionals should not be about performance review. They should be about development, examining strengths and weaknesses, planning for the future, etc; but essentially non-objectified work activities should not be artificially made objective. Using such a system is invalid.

THE PROBLEM WITH STAFF APPRAISAL

It has been argued that appraisal is one of the seven deadly sins afflicting managers (only six others?) because it inappropriately attributes variation in performance to the individual employee rather than to problems higher up the organisational ladder. The effect of this is to shift the blame for problems onto individual workers rather than look at what is wrong with the way the organisation is set up and run. Hopefully by discussing how appraisal should be integrated into the organisation, and how the open organisation can recognise organisational issues, this problem can be reduced.

The problem of the organisation can jeopardise not only the appraisal system itself, but the morale of the workforce, particularly if they feel they are being unfairly criticised. If this happens, the main reasons for having the appraisal system, to maximise the job satisfaction of the employee and productivity, will be lost.

In order to be effective, the appraisal system must take into account the philosophy and structure of the organisation.

If the 360 degree appraisal is used, it has to be fully integrated into the organisation; both managers and workers must believe in the system and the organisation and then it can be effective.

CONCLUSIONS

If the guidelines laid out in this book are followed, then appraisal will perform a useful function for both employees and employers. On the other hand, appraisals have little value if they are not designed properly, and if the individuals taking part do not believe in the organisation or the appraisal system itself. If the appraisal system is not valid, then the organisation is simply throwing money away, wasting time and resources on a system that is not doing what it is supposed to, optimise job satisfaction and organisational efficiency.

The appraisal is a method of assessing the role of the individual in the organisation. There are two main purposes: to ensure that employees have maximised job satisfaction and fulfilment, and to ensure that the right person is in the right job and doing it to a suitable standard.

Too many appraisal systems only consider the latter point, at best paying lip-service to the former. In modern society there is a growing awareness of the value of people, that they mean more than short-term profit. The open organisation will truly recognise the importance of this.

Glossary

Aptitude An ability relating to a specific task or area of knowledge to do with the job (eg sales aptitude, mechanical aptitude).

Bias Acting more favourably towards one person or group than another without good reason. Bias is common, and needs to be protected against. Simply being aware of the existence of bias and actively attempting to minimise its effects is beneficial. Validation of the appraisal system will determine the extent and type of bias. It is critical to try avoid bias, though this can be difficult, partly because much of the information relating to the appraisal is subjective and because appraisers and appraisees tend to know each other well as they work together on a daily basis.

Career development One primary aim of the appraisal is to ensure that the appraisee's future within the organisation is being properly planned, that it is progressing in a satisfactory manner. The appraisal is an opportunity for individuals to express any dissatisfaction and to make suggestions (eg transfer or training).

Communication The act of conveying information between two or more parties. Effective communication in the appraisal is essential. All relevant information should be received at the right time by both parties.

Conflict Conflict is unavoidable in some appraisals. It is sometimes related to the job and sometimes to the people involved. Conflict arises when there is a discrepancy between the needs of the organisation and the needs of the individual. Appraisal is important in reducing conflict.

Correlation A statistical technique used to determine the degree of relationship or association between two variables. The closer the relationship the higher the correlation. A perfect positive correlation is $+1.0$; a perfect negative correlation -1.0. If there is no relationship the correlation is 0.

Counselling Counselling is used by organisations as they recognise it has useful purposes, from reducing stress to the analysis of personal problems. The organisation should not use counselling as a solution to problems arising out of the work situation. A good organisation will ensure that the causes of the problems are addressed. Counselling involves listening to the individual, empathising with their situation and helping them to work through their problems in their own way.

Data (quantitative/qualitative) Data are the information collected for use in the appraisal. Quantitative data are numerical information, perhaps in the form of rating scales or psychometric test results. Qualitative data are usually in verbal or written form. They are non-quantifiable. Both kinds of data are open to bias and problems of interpretation if not used carefully.

Discrimination This refers to the systematic differential treatment of groups of people, with prejudicial connotations. There are many forms of discrimination, some of which are recognised by law, eg race, sex, disability. Appraisers should be aware of other forms of discrimination which are not recognised by law, eg style of speech, attitudes to life – things which can be difficult to define (see **bias**).

Feedback The appraisee should receive information relating to their performance not just after the appraisal interview but throughout the year. Feedback should be constructive, and should focus on both good (praise/reward) and poor (constructive criticism) performance.

Follow up The concrete results of the appraisal, the decisions made to take action of some sort, such as training. Without follow up the appraisal is meaningless.

Future potential What is the individual likely to achieve in the future: in which areas are they likely to be successful? An appraisal to assess future potential is often carried out shortly after an individual joins the organisation to see how to best satisfy personal and organisational needs. Such appraisals should be carried out regularly.

Intelligence General mental ability, as opposed to specific aptitudes. Intelligence is the ability to adapt effectively to novel situations. Intelligence can predict performance in many situations.

Interview Interviewing is used in any situation where people wish to receive and give verbal information in an orderly fashion, and to discuss issues of importance (eg selection and appraisal).

Interviewing skills An interview is more than just a chat. The success or otherwise of the interview depends on the type of questions asked and the responses received. Both interviewers and interviewees should give a lot of thought to what they are going to say.

Job analysis The determination of what the job actually entails. There is a range of methods used to analyse jobs, including observation, interviews, questionnaires and task analysis.

Job description All jobs should have an accurate, detailed, and up-to-date job description so workers are clear about their duties and responsibilities and their role within the organisation.

Job redesign This involves restructuring the job, perhaps after problems or issues have emerged through job analysis. Tasks may be altered, added or removed in order to create a more coherent job, and maximise the efficiency and satisfaction of workers carrying out the job. It should be carried out in consultation with job-holders, supervisors and anyone else involved in the job.

Job satisfaction In previous decades, organisations have focused on maximising productivity. Now many are also concerned with the welfare of their employees, which in turn benefits the organisation.

Leadership This is crucial to organisational success. The best leaders share certain qualities; they tend to be sociable, extroverted, considerate towards others, assertive and intuitive. They are not necessarily more intelligent than the rest of the workers, but they can create and maintain group cohesion and give direction and purpose to group activities. But effective leadership is more than having the right personal qualities, the ethos of the organisation is also important.

Listening skills Crucial to any appraiser. In order to listen properly one must be listening actively and genuinely, empathising with the speaker and making appropriate comments.

Motivation The 'whys' behind people's actions. People behave in certain ways because they have certain needs. These can be basic physiological needs such as food, warmth and shelter; or psychological needs such as companionship and personal growth. In many work environments it is usually the psychological needs that require attention.

Negotiation This concerns the rules of discussion that are involved when two people with differing initial positions try to reach a compromise acceptable to both.

Objectives/targets Employees perform better when they know what they need to achieve. Targets are often difficult to set. They can be difficult to quantify (eg for managers and professionals), or difficult to set at a reasonable level, one neither impossible to reach nor too easy – both of which may demotivate the employee.

Open organisation A forward thinking way of running an organisation. The open organisation maximises autonomy for the individual through freedom of action and consultation. The open organisation recognises that people perform best when they are respected as individuals and their views are taken into account within the organisation.

Peer ratings These are gaining in popularity though they should be used with caution. They arose because individuals who work together know a great deal about each other's performance. Ratings should be confidential and anonymous. There is a danger that some people might indulge in the airing of personal grievances.

Performance criteria Criteria should be objective and quantifiable if possible. They should be used and interpreted with care. When used appropriately they are very useful in the appraisal. Bear in mind performance is often dependent not only on the individual, but on the organisation.

Performance review The process of estimating the value of an individual to the organisation through regular assessment. It often forms an important part of the appraisal.

Person specification The theoretically ideal person for a particular job. The specification includes a number of categories, such as intelligence, aptitudes and personality, and qualifications.

Personality Relatively permanent ways of behaving which characterise individuals and make them different from others. The differences are called 'traits', eg extroversion, aggression, neuroticism. Personality, when measured accurately, can be a good predictor of performance in elements of the job, such as teamworking or assessing training needs.

Psychometric tests Psychometric measures can provide detailed objective information on abilities, personality and interests very quickly. Measures are accurate predictors of how an individual will perform in various circumstances.

Reliability Any assessment device (eg psychometric measure, interview, appraisal system as a whole) should provide consistent, stable findings if used to measure the same thing on two or more occasions, or used with two or more people.

Reviewer Alternative name for appraiser, used in the performance review.

Supervisor A broad term meaning anyone responsible for one or more people within the organisation. The notion of authority is difficult to assess. In some circumstances the supervisor has a great deal of authority. This should not be the case in an open organisation.

Supervisor ratings One of the commonest forms of data used in the appraisal. They are also one of the most abused techniques. The development of appropriate scales is a complex activity. Good scales provide very useful information.

Task analysis Part of job analysis. The task analysis determines the number and types of tasks involved in the job, the frequency with which they are carried out, and the percentage of time spent on the task.

Training One of the most important outcomes of the appraisal. The analysis of training needs is a crucial part of appraisal. There is little point in looking at a person's deficiencies if this information is not acted on, and acted on quickly. The costs of training are usually quickly recouped.

Upward ratings Ratings completed by people who are supervised by the appraisee. A relatively new idea, these can provide valuable information about the performance of the appraisee from the perspective of colleagues.

Validation A good appraisal system will always have defects. Validation is systematic analysis involving analysis of the system to discover any defects and to find ways of rectifying them.

Validity The extent to which something is accurate and useful in a particular situation.

Useful addresses

Advisory, Conciliation and Arbitration Service (ACAS)
Brandon House
180 Borough High Street
London SE1 1LW
www.acas.org.uk

British Chambers of Commerce
65 Petty France
St James Park
London SW1H 9EU
www.chamberonline.co.uk

British Education Management and Administration Society
BELMAS Office
Sheffield Hallam University
Collegiate Crescent
Sheffield S10 2BP

British Psychological Society
St Andrews House
48 Princess Road East
Leicester LE1 7DR
www.bps.org.uk

Career Analysts
Career House
90 Gloucester Place
London W1U 6BL
www.careeranalysts.co.uk

Chartered Institute for Personnel and Development
CIPD House
Camp Road
London SW19 4UX
www.cipd.co.uk

Chartered Management Institute
3rd Floor
2 Savoy Court
Strand
London WC2R 0EZ
www.managers.org.uk/institute/home_3.asp

Commission for Racial Equality
Elliott House
10/12 Arlington Street
London SW1E 5WH
www.cre.gov.uk

Confederation of British Industry
Centre Point
103 New Oxford Street
London WC1A 1DU
www.cbi.org.uk/home.html

Data Protection Registrar
Information Commissioner's Office
Wycliffe House
Water Lane
Wilmslow
Cheshire SK9 5AX
www.informationcommissioner.gov.uk/eventual.
  aspx?id-1

Department of Trade and Industry
DTI Enquiry Unit
1 Victoria Street
London SW1H 0ET
www.dti.gov.uk

Equal Opportunities Commission
Arndale House
Arndale Centre
Manchester M4 3EQ
www.eoc.org.uk

The Institute of Employment Rights
177 Abbeville Road
London SW4 9RL
www.ier.org.uk

Institute of Management Consultancy
3rd Floor
17–18 Hayward's Place
London EC1R 0EQ
www.imc.co.uk

Index

360 degree appraisal, 11,
    133–152
  benefits, 140–141
  practicalities, 143–147
  problems and solutions,
    147 151
  validity, 146–147
  who should not use it?,
    141–143
  who should use it?, 137–140

ability tests, 169
appraisal,
  continuous, 131
  failure, 38
  form, 194–196
  officer, 68
  pay-related, 118–122
  purposes, 41–65
  regular, 131–132
  skills, 66–95
  timing, 43, 131–132
  what goes wrong, 13–17
appraiser, 67–71
aptitude, 104, 110, 112–113,
    169–170, 232

background information,
    77–78
Behaviourally-Anchored
    Rating Scales, 162–165
Belbin, 124–128
bias, 32–33, 232
British Psychological Society,
    168

career development, 232
change, 35–36
commitment, 37–38
communication, 78, 232
conflict, 233
conflict resolution, 196
conflict, sources, 216–217
correlation, 233
counselling skills, 80–81, 233
criticism, constructive, 90–91,
    190–191

data, 90, 173–174, 233
design, 12–13
discrimination, 233–234

empathy, 76

encouragement, 72
ethical issues, 11–12, 225
evaluation, 200–219

feedback, 234
follow up, 202–204, 234
future potential, 234

halo effect, 215–216
health, 56–58

intelligence, 234
interest questionnaire,
    171–172
interview, 182–199, 234
    afterwards, 193–197
    closure, 191
    conducting, 187–191
    place, 186–187
    preparation, 78–80,182–183
    purposes of, 76–77
    questions, 80
    scheduling, 183–186
    skills, 73–74, 235
    structure, 187–189

job analysis, 88–90, 99–101,
    235
job description, 97–99,
    105–108, 114–117, 151,
    197, 235
job redesign, 59–60, 235
job satisfaction, 235
judgement, objective, 92

leadership, 235–236
legal issues, 225
listening skills, 74–76, 236

motivation, 30, 43–44, 110,
    113, 236
    questionnaire, 172

negotiating skills, 81–88, 236

objectives, 61, 165–167, 236
open organisation, 9–10,
    20–40, 236
    autonomy, 31–32
    available information,
        25–27
    secrecy, 28–29
    transparency, 27–28
organisation, size of, 8–9

peer appraisal, 124–128
peer ratings, 237
performance criteria,
    154–157, 237
performance-related pay,
    34–35, 49, 118–122
performance review, 45–50,
    237
personality, 104, 110, 113,
    237
    questionnaire, 170–171
person specification, 108–114,
    114–117, 151, 237
potential, 53–54
praise, 49–50, 72–73, 190–191

pre-appraisal report, 79, 174–177
preparation, 72, 78–80, 153–181, 177, 179–181
problems, 61–63, 192–193, 229–230
psychometric measures, 167–173, 237–238
purpose of appraisal, 3–4
problems of appraisal, 5–6
promotion, 52–53

questionnaires, 92

ratings, 158–165
system, 161–162
rating scales, 92
reliability, 238
reviewer, 238

self-appraisal, 122–123
stereotyping, 213
supervisor, 238
supervisor ratings, 238

task analysis, 102–104, 238
teams, 124–128
development, 58–59
training, 8, 50–52, 190, 202–203, 238

unfairness, 212–216
upward appraisal, 128–130, 239

validity, 205–212, 239
vocational guidance, 55–56

work-home balance, 57–58, 224